MW01708692

In Those Days, At This Time

In Those Days, At This Time

Holiness and History in the Jewish Calendar

by Eliezer Segal

University of Calgary Press

University of Calgary Press
2500 University Drive NW
Calgary, Alberta
Canada T2N 1N4
www.uofcpress.com

LIBRARY AND ARCHIVES CANADA CATALOGUING IN PUBLICATION

Segal, Eliezer
In those days, at this time : holiness and history in the Jewish calendar / Eliezer Segal.

Includes bibliographical references and index.
ISBN 978-1-55238-185-4

1. Fasts and feasts–Judaism. I. Title.

BM690.S45 2006 296.4'3 C2006-901033-1

The University of Calgary Press acknowledges the support of the Alberta Foundation for the Arts for our publications. We acknowledge the financial support of the Government of Canada through the Book Publishing Industry Development Program (BPIDP) for our publishing activities. We acknowledge the financial support of the Canada Council for the Arts for our publishing program.

Canada | Canada Council for the Arts | Conseil des Arts du Canada | Alberta Foundation for the Arts

Printed and bound in Canada by AGMV Marquis
This book is printed on FSC Silva Enviro paper

Cover design by Melina Cusano
Page design and typesetting by Jessica Maier

Table of Contents

Introduction

In his eloquent tribute to the Sabbath*, Abraham Joshua Heschel wrote:

> *Judaism is a religion of time. Unlike the space-minded man to whom time is unvaried, iterative, homogeneous, to whom all hours are alike, qualitiless, empty shells, the Bible senses the diversified character of time. There are no two hours alike. Every hour is unique and the only one given at any moment, exclusive and endlessly precious.*
>
> *Judaism teaches us to be attached to holiness in time, to be attached to sacred events, to learn how to consecrate sanctuaries that emerge from the magnificent stream of a year.... Jewish ritual may be characterized as the art of significant forms in time, as architecture of time.... The main themes of faith lie in the realm of time.*

---

* Heschel, Abraham Joshua. *The Earth Is the Lord's and the Sabbath*, Harper Torchbooks Temple Library. New York: Harper & Row, 1966, p. 8.

A conclusion that may be drawn from Heschel's perceptive observation is that there is no better way of describing the intricacies of the Jewish religious tradition than by focusing on the rhythms of its sacred calendar. The weekly Sabbath, as well as the assorted annual festivals of pilgrimage, historical commemoration, appreciation of natural rhythms or spiritual regeneration – all of these have drawn the unceasing attention of diverse types of Jews belonging to different eras, lands, and ideological persuasions. On the one hand, the themes and symbols of the ancient holy days (which have been supplemented occasionally by the introduction of new days of historical commemoration) have been continually reinterpreted or appreciated in novel ways, so that they have never lost their enduring relevance to Jews. On the other hand, the infinite range of human personalities, values, and social circumstances have found expression through the ways in which they have come into relation with the Jewish festival cycle.

The present volume is not intended to serve as an introduction to the Jewish religious calendar, and certainly not as a learned monograph on that topic, absorbing as such a study might be. There is no scarcity of books that survey the Jewish holidays from assorted religious or scholarly perspectives. My purpose here is not so much to instill a deeper knowledge of the holidays as it is to use those holidays as a prism through which to illuminate the immeasurable varieties of the Jewish experience. We shall have ample opportunities, in the course of our meandering excursion across Jewish sacred time, to appreciate how occasions that might appear on the surface to be days of straightforward agricultural or historical commemoration can also become venues for encounters between rationalism and superstition, messianism and mysticism, universality and parochialism, art and commerce, modernity and tradition, passion and intellect.

Jewish tradition insists that an appropriate blessing should accompany each religious deed. In this way, the worshipper is made conscious of the spiritual dimension of what might otherwise have been no more than a physical or secular activity. On historical festivals such as Hanukkah and Purim, which celebrate the rescue of the Jewish people from physical or spiritual threats, one of the prescribed blessings is: "Blessed are you, Lord, our God, sovereign of the universe, who has performed miracles for our ancestors in those days, at this time."

The plain meaning of the closing phrase "at this time" is merely that the date of the particular festival is the anniversary of the ancient event that is being commemorated. There is, however, something about the wording that suggests to me an additional lesson; namely that the events of the past can never be detached from our present situation. History, no matter how remote in years, is not something that can be relegated to a distant age. Rather, it should be appreciated as a living force that continues to shape our relationships with the present and the future.

In Those Days, at This Time is a natural sequel to its predecessor, *Holidays, History and Halakhah*, published by Jason Aronson Publishers. Like its predecessor, this book grew out of my journalistic commitment to providing material appropriate for holiday editions of the respective publications to which I have contributed. The vast majority of the chapters first appeared in *The Jewish Free Press* in my hometown of Calgary, Alberta.

This collection, no less than the previous ones, attests to my fascination with Jewish history and tradition and my conviction that old Jewish documents can be relevant to out contemporary situation. My stimulating experiences in a Department of Religious Studies have convinced me that many of the phenomena that I once regarded as distinctive or idiosyncratic to the Jewish experience are in reality shared by other cultures and religious communities. I have made especial efforts to point out such instances, which are often rooted in fundamental truths of human nature and social dynamics. In presenting this material, is my sincere hope that experience will be entertaining no less than it is educating.

Several of the chapters in this book were written during that stimulating academic sabbatical year of 1999–2000, which I spent in Jerusalem enjoying convenient access to the bibliographical treasures of the Jewish National and University Library. That sabbatical was facilitated and enhanced by a generous grant from the Lady Davis Fellowship Trust, to which I wish to express my gratitude.

The target audiences envisaged for this book consist chiefly of a Jewish laity (who were the readers of the original newspaper articles) or individuals with a basic background in world religions. Either group would be expected to be familiar with most of the Hebrew terminology (words like *halakhah*, *mitzvah*, and so forth) and historical references (Rashi, Talmud, etc.). In order to make it accessible to a broader readership, I have added brief introductions to each chapter, in which I outline the main features of the respective holidays, as well as an extensive alphabetical glossary at the end of the book where the curious reader may conveniently find explanations of specialist terms and identifications of persons or works mentioned in the volume.

For more advanced or ambitious readers, references to classical biblical, talmudic, and other ancient sources have been inserted into the text.

The Sabbath

The Jewish Sabbath [Hebrew: Shabbat] is rooted in the biblical command to observe every Saturday (beginning Friday at sunset) by refraining from creative labour, in acknowledgment of the belief that God created the universe in six days and ceased on the seventh, and as an assertion of freedom from slavery. This day of rest and spiritual regeneration is defined, among other things, by abstention from profane activities, and by numerous special prayers and rituals.

You Have Mail!*

The many restrictions that define the traditional Jewish Sabbath are not necessarily to everyone's taste. I have found, however, that there is one feature that rarely fails to impress people who have had no previous experience of Sabbath observance in the modern world.

I am referring to the ability to ignore the ringing of a telephone.

In watching an Orthodox Jew sit nonchalantly as the nudnik appliance keeps crying out for attention, we can appreciate how enslaved we were to it during the other days of the week. Ironically, the aspects of Shabbat observance that involve non-use of electricity are, of course, modern innovations that have no clear precedents in ancient or medieval Judaism. While a virtual consensus has developed regarding the *fact* of the prohibition, the rabbis are not all that clear when it comes to explaining its reason. Nevertheless, being unplugged is probably the single most conspicuous identifier of the Biblical Day of Rest for observant Jews today.

* *The Jewish Free Press*, Calgary, September 14, 2000, p. 14.

Though earlier generations did not have to deal with the demands of the telephone, they did have to cope with written mail and with the question of whether it could be read on the Sabbath. The Talmud (*Shabbat* 16b) cites a ruling that one should not read "profane documents" on the holy day, and the later commentators were in disagreement about what kinds of documents were included in this prohibition.

Rashi initially supported a broad definition that encompassed not only commercial bills and the like, which are obviously inappropriate on the day of rest, but also simple personal correspondence. Rashi's students challenged his interpretation, noting that it did not reflect the widespread practice. Rabbi Isaac of Dampierre pointed out that a newly arrived letter might possibly contain urgent matters involving life-or-death issues, and hence it should be permissible to open and read it. Rashi's grandson Rabbi Jacob Tam took this reasoning a step further, and argued that if the recipient was already familiar with the contents of the letter (for example, if it had arrived and been read earlier in the week), then re-reading it on the Sabbath would not actually accomplish anything, and therefore cannot be defined as a act of labour that could be forbidden on the Sabbath.

As cited in the *Tosafot* commentary to the Talmud, the authorities make it clear that the point of their controversy is limited to correspondence, where a reasonable likelihood exists that its contents will have some measure of urgency. However, by no means do they consider permitting as Sabbath reading material "those war epics composed in the vernacular" – that is, works like the *Chanson de Roland* and other troubadour romances and tales of chivalry that enjoyed popularity among the Jewish readership. In fact, the *Tosafot* add wryly, "Rabbi Isaac did not know who allowed such works to be read on weekdays."

In a society where most of our communications are conducted by means of the telephone or other electronic media, it is doubtful if most of us (other than physicians, police or other emergency workers) would consider seriously the chances that any snail-mail message might be critically urgent. Nevertheless, persistent ringing might impel some individuals to pick up the telephone receiver just in case.

A rabbi's son once related to me such an experience, when the unceasing ringing of the telephone, into the late hours of Friday night finally persuaded his father to answer the phone on the assumption that the call was about a life-or-death emergency.

As it turned out, at the other end of the line was a congregant who wanted the address of a Jewish publisher.

That incident was considerably more benign than the ordeals faced by students of Martin Buber. The celebrated existentialist philosopher was so hostile to the observance of religious law – which, he felt, placed barriers in the way of a direct I-Thou relationship with the Almighty – that he could not stomach the fact that several of his most distinguished and devoted disciples were traditionally observant Jews.

One of those students, the eminent educational philosopher Akiva Ernst Simon, had a policy of answering the telephone on the Sabbath if it rang more than fifteen times, which constituted sufficient proof for him that the matter was urgent. Unfortunately, Buber was aware of Simon's policy, and made it his custom to periodically telephone his student on Shabbat, ringing persistently until he was answered, and then he would mockingly chastise him for picking up the receiver.

Compared to the problems posed by today's telephones and e-mails, Rashi and the other rabbis of earlier times had an easy time of it deciding whether or not to read newly arrived letters. Lacking all the distractions of our Information Age, they could find the time and concentration to produce commentaries and responsa that had truly lasting worth.

Suggestions for Further Reading

Diamond, Malcolm L. *Martin Buber: Jewish Existentialist,* Harper Torchbooks. New York and Evanston: Harper & Row, 1968.

Simon, Ernst. "Martin Buber: His Way between Thought and Deed," *Jewish Frontier* (February 1948): 25.

———. "Martin Buber and the Faith of Israel," *Iyyun: Hebrew Philosophical Quarterly* 9, no. 1 (1958): 13–50.

Rosh Hashanah and Yom Kippur

Rosh Hashanah [New Years], celebrated in the fall, has its roots in the vague biblical injunction to observe a day of "sounding the shofar [ram's horn]" on the first day of the seventh Hebrew month. In subsequent Jewish tradition, the day is perceived as a universal Day of Judgment on which God assesses people's deeds and determines their fates for the coming year.

Yom Kippur [the Day of Atonement], on the tenth day of the month, is marked by fasting and abstention from physical pleasures, as the community prays that their sins will be forgiven and that any negative verdict be cancelled.

These two holy days are at the heart of a powerful penitential season, in which Jews strive to repent, abandoning their past sins and determined to improve their moral and spiritual states.

Dancing with the Demons*

A recurring question in the Talmud (*Berakhot* 13a, etc.) concerns the need for conscious intention in the performance of religious precepts. Though everyone would agree that we should initially strive to be fully mindful of our actions, there is still room to ask: What is the *de facto* status of a mitzvah (commandment) that was performed under compulsion or absentmindedly? Is the performance deemed adequate, or must it be done all over again?

Depending on the precise nature of each commandment and the wording of its biblical proof-text, different rulings are applied to different cases. Predictably, there are occasional disputes among the rabbis about how to interpret the sources.

The Talmud (*Rosh Hashanah* 27b–28a) raises this issue in connection with the sounding of the shofar on Rosh Hashanah. As usual, it attempts to translate the theoretical considerations into a concrete case, as follows: What is the status of a person who sounds the shofar "in

* *The Jewish Free Press*, Calgary, September 17, 1998, pp. 20–21.

song," as a mere musical instrument? Has such a person fulfilled the religious obligation on Rosh Hashanah?

In explaining the passage, Rashi's commentary adds the following remark: "In the text of my teacher Rabbi Isaac ben Judah I have seen the reading 'if one sounds it for *a demon*'; that is to say, in order to drive away an evil spirit."

The textual variation between "song" and "demon" is, after all, a barely perceptible one in an unvocalized Hebrew text. The words "le-shir" and "le-shed" differ only by a *dalet* and a *resh,* which are graphically almost identical. Either reading provides a valid instance of how someone could blow a shofar without intending to fulfill the religious precept.

Further investigation reveals that the divergence in the talmudic texts predates Rashi and his teachers by several generations. The matter is discussed by Rav Hai Ga'on, who headed the Babylonian academy of Pumbedita in the tenth century. Rav Hai reports: "Our reading is 'in song'; such as to accompany the psalm that is sung over the offering of a sacrifice, or to make music.... However we have heard that there are those in the academy of Mehasiah who have the reading 'for a demon'.... At any rate, we have no idea how or why a person would sound a shofar for such creatures."

This last remark has an unmistakable tone of ironic sarcasm, expressive of the longstanding academic rivalry that frequently coloured the relations between those two foremost institutions of Jewish learning whose origins can be traced to the third century. The yeshivahs of

Pumbedita and Mata Mehasiah – the latter is better known by its other name "Sura" – were the principal venues for the debates of the Babylonian Talmud, and they continued to co-exist through the Islamic era (though then they moved to the new metropolis of Baghdad).

Rav Hai's derisive dismissal of the "demon" tradition in the Talmud text is consistent with a fundamental divergence in the religious outlooks of the two Babylonian academies, one that continues to surface throughout the talmudic and Ge'onic eras. While the Pumbeditans were distinguished by their rationalism, the Suran rabbis had a reputation for delving into magic and the supernatural. There is no small measure of irony in the fact that Rav Hai himself acquired a posthumous reputation as a mystic, the result of spurious traditions that were ascribed to him by later generations.

Thus, among the revered scholars of Sura we find the ninth-century Ga'on Rabbi Moses Hakohen, famous for his expertise in amulets and spells. Shortly afterward, the story goes, the Ga'on Rav Natronai of Sura transported himself magically from Babylonia to Spain and back again in order to teach Torah, without taking a caravan and without being observed in any conventional mode of transportation. This episode was often invoked by the proud Spanish Jews as evidence of the antiquity and authority of their scholarly tradition.

When Rav Hai Ga'on was asked to comment on Natronai's legendary exploit, he treated it with his customary skepticism: "Stuff and nonsense!" he assured the

Jews of Kairowan, Tunisia. "Perhaps it was just some impostor who showed up claiming to be Rav Natronai."

Though he insisted that the reports of Rav Moses Hakohen's magical abilities were greatly exaggerated, Rav Hai admitted that similar beliefs were popular in Sura. This should not be surprising, since they dwell in close proximity to the Babylonians and the House of Nebuchadnezzar, and have been influenced by their pagan superstitions. Not so for the enlightened sages of Pumbedita who have never been tainted by such folly.

The moral of the story, concludes Rav Hai, is that a fool will believe everything he is told!

Both the Suran and the Pumbeditan approaches had their followers among subsequent generations of Jews. In spite of Rav Hai's professed perplexity about the purpose of sounding the shofar for a demon, it is a well established rabbinic belief that one of the objectives of the shofar is to "confuse Satan" when he rises to accuse us before the Heavenly Court (*Rosh Hashanah* 16b). Many Jewish thinkers have been quick to insist that such imagery must be understood metaphorically, although others (like Maimonides) omitted that explanation altogether.

However there have also been Jews who believed with stark literalness in the efficacy of the shofar as a weapon against demonic forces. This was particularly true among the Jews of Central and Eastern Europe, who had less exposure to scientific and philosophical rationalism than their cousins in the Arabic-speaking world.

Thus it happened one Rosh Hashanah in medieval Frankfort that the community's shofar could not be made to utter a sound, and the congregation had no doubt of the cause: Satan was sitting inside the ram's horn! Once the problem had been diagnosed, the remedy was a simple one: Psalm 91, long acknowledged as a potent defence against evil spirits, was recited three times into the haunted shofar, and immediately it became usable.

Hopefully, the sounding of the shofar will be received neither as musical entertainment nor as protection against demons, but rather as a meaningful call to improve our spiritual and moral lives for the coming year.

Suggestions for Further Reading

Asaf, S. *Tequfat ha-Ge'onim ve-Sifrutah.* Jerusalem: Mossad Harav Kook, 1967.

Trachtenberg, Joshua. *Jewish Magic and Superstition: A Study in Folk Religion. Temple Books.* New York: Atheneum, 1970.

Roman Holiday*

It was the night of Rosh Hashanah, in the year 5040 (1280). For Rabbi Abraham Abulafia this was the perfect time to pay a call on the Pope.

Abulafia was one of the most bizarre and colourful figures in Jewish history. A native of Spain, he set out toward the Middle East at the age of twenty in search of the fabled Sambation River, whose rock-heaving waters presented an insurmountable barrier to the return of the ten lost tribes of Israel. When this project failed, he continued his travels in Greece and Italy.

Abulafia concocted a unique mystical discipline that wove together elements from the Kabbalah, Aristotelian philosophy, and yoga-like meditation. He believed that through the pursuit of this regimen he could aspire to prophetic revelations.

And it almost goes without saying that such an eccentric eventually became convinced that he was the messiah.

---

* *The Jewish Free Press*, Calgary, September 9, 1999, p. 24.

In most of Abulafia's writings, he seems to portray the messianic vocation in rather modest dimensions. All individuals can become messiahs insofar as they can bring about a spiritual liberation of their own souls.

Nevertheless, the conventional perception of the messiah as a national redeemer was not absent from Abulafia's self-image.

In keeping with the prevailing views of the time, this made it virtually mandatory that he have an audience with the leader of the Christian church.

Centuries of Jewish literature had elaborated the idea of an ultimate confrontation between the Jewish redeemer and the presiding chief of the evil empire. Whereas ancient texts regarded the pagan Roman Empire as the ultimate foe, many medievals believed that this role had been inherited by the oppressive Roman church.

This expectation had been given explicit formulation in recent years by Rabbi Moses Nahmanides, who had declared, in his disputation with the apostate Pablo Christiani, in Barcelona 1264, that "when the final time arrives, the messiah will approach the Pope at God's command, and say 'Let my people go that they may worship me!' Only then will he have truly arrived."

Evidently it was with such thoughts in his mind that Abulafia (who preferred to designate himself by the mystical title "Raziel") was inspired to seek his audience with the pontiff on that fateful Rosh Hashanah.

The aspiring messiah did not conceal his plans, and it did not take long for Pope Martin to receive word of his distinguished visitor. The Pope gave orders to the Vatican staff that if the rabbi should drop in seeking to discuss Judaism with him, they should arrest him immediately and send him to a place outside the city where the firewood was already prepared for a quick execution. Though Abulafia was notified in advance of the Pope's inhospitable intentions, he remained determined nonetheless to keep his appointment.

And thus it was that he approached the gates of the Vatican on that foreboding Rosh Hashanah eve.

And at that moment, the announcement was made that Pope Martin had passed away at the ripe age of eighty. Abulafia's life was saved.

Needless to say, the good rabbi interpreted this development as divine intervention and as irrefutable proof of the authenticity of his mission – notwithstanding the fact that he was imprisoned for a month by Franciscan monks.

More than two centuries later, another self-styled Jewish redeemer was planning a trip to Rome. The individual in question was David Reubeni, a mysterious adventurer who claimed to be the brother of the monarch of an independent Jewish kingdom in Arabia.

Masquerading as a descendant of the Islamic prophet, he wandered through Ethiopia, Egypt, and Israel. It was while sojourning in Alexandria in 5284 (1523) that he spent Rosh Hashanah in a small synagogue awaiting the next available ship to Italy.

It would take more than two months to find a galley sailing to Venice, and more than a year before he would enter the Papal palace on a white steed. Pope Clement greeted David with full diplomatic honours when the Hebrew emissary proposed a strategic alliance between his kingdom, Rome, and Portugal, such that a Jewish army would expel the Turks from the Holy Land. Clement even provided David with letters of introduction to several European rulers. With these documents in hand, he came close to finalizing a pact with the Portuguese king for the transporting of armaments to Reubeni's fictitious regiments.

So impressive were David Reubeni's exploits among the European elites that a young Converso Jew named Diego Pires was inspired to return openly to Judaism, taking the name of Solomon Molkho.

Convincing himself that he was the messiah, Solomon journeyed to Turkey, Israel, and Italy, and of course he eventually arrived in Rome for the obligatory confrontation with the Pope. The pontiff extended to him hospitality and protection.

When it became impossible to resist the Inquisition's persistent calls for Molkho's death, it is stated that Pope Clement saved his life by substituting a condemned criminal to be executed in his stead. Eventually however, Solomon became unable to fend off his accusers. He was arrested by the Holy Roman Emperor Charles V and perished as a martyr, proudly proclaiming his Judaism to the end.

David Reubeni, who was imprisoned along with his disciple, managed somehow to evade death, and lived out the rest of his days in a Spanish prison under Imperial protection.

A Jewish chronicler reports that even after Molkho's demise there remained many Jews who were convinced that the aspiring messiah had miraculously cheated death, and that eight days after the *auto-da-fé* he had been seen at his home.

When Shabbetai Zvi, the mystical messianic figure of the seventeenth century, achieved prominence throughout the Jewish world, he spent his entire career in Turkey and the Holy Land and did not make any attempt to visit the Vatican. Nevertheless, the Pope could not ignore the momentous events of the age, particularly after he received anxious letters from clergy in Jerusalem who were convinced that a Jewish restoration was imminent and that Christians faced a threat of expulsion. He was compelled to send a fact-finding delegation to keep a close eye on the developments.

In 1668, following Shabbetai Zvi's conversion to Islam, the aspiring messiah sent his "prophet," Nathan of Gaza, on a special mission to Rome to perform a mysterious ritual whose purpose was to purify the Vatican, symbolically imprisoning the "Prince of Edom" and binding him in chains. His journeys through the Jewish communities of Italy served as a catalyst for the eruption of factionalist controversies between the messianists and their opponents. At length, perhaps in gentile disguises, Nathan was able to spend a few days in Rome, where he performed his secret rituals, felling the metaphysical princes of evil by means of the power of the divine name. Unfortunately, he was eventually defeated by the demonic forces against which he was battling. Shabbetai Zvi reproached Nathan for the failure of his mission, and sent him to wage another spiritual battle in the Balkans, where his movement was more safely established.

Abraham Abulafia's planned Rosh Hashanah visit with Pope Martin should therefore be seen as a link in a distinguished series of such encounters. If only we possessed the precise text of the message that the Jewish mystic intended to deliver to the Christian leader.

I hope, at least, that Abulafia had the good grace to wish the pope a cordial "Gut Yontef, Pontiff."

Suggestions for Further Reading

Benayahu, M. "The Shabatean Movement in Greece," *Sefunot* 14 (The Book of Greek Jewry) (1971–77): 9–555.

Scholem, G. G. *Ha-Qabbalah Shel Sefer ha-Temunah veshel Avraham Abulafia*, Jerusalem: Akademon, 1972.

———. *Sabbatai Sevi, the Mystical Messiah, 1626–1676, Bollingen Series*, Princeton: Princeton University Press, 1973.

Schwartz, Leo W. *Memoirs of My People: Jewish Self-Portraits from the 11th to the 20th Centuries*, New York: Schocken, 1963.

Where to Draw the Line*

Our God and God of our fathers, reign thou in thy glory over the whole world, and be exalted above all the earth in thine honour, and shine forth in the splendour and excellence of thy might upon all the inhabitants of thy world....

These stirring phrases from the New Years Musaf prayer illustrate aptly the universalistic tone of the High Holy Day season, a feature that sets it apart from all other periods in the Jewish calendar.

The resolve of Jews to observe their traditions in lands and climes far from Jerusalem presents some unique and intriguing challenges to the custodians of Jewish law.

Although the dates for all the Jewish holidays can now be conveniently ascertained, even years in advance, by consulting a calendar, this was not the case during talmudic times.

* *Ha-Atid: Magazine of the Melbourne Hebrew Congregation*, Melbourne Australia: August–October 1999, 3:4: 67–68.

According to the astronomical cycles, the appearance of the new moon could take place either twenty-nine or thirty days after the commencement of the preceding month. The precise date had to be determined on each occasion by a properly constituted court in Jerusalem, on the basis of testimony from witnesses who had actually observed the relevant astronomical phenomena. Only then could the start of the new month be officially declared. Messengers would then be dispatched to publicize that decision, and until the arrival of those messengers, distant Jewish communities could not be certain exactly when to observe any festivals that might occur during the month.

Although a perpetual computed calendar was introduced in the fourth century, traditional Jews outside the Holy Land have continued to add an extra day to most festivals, a vestige of those earlier times when the messengers would not have reached their localities in time to notify them of the correct date.

Rosh Hashanah remains the only festival for which the extra day is observed even in Israel. As the only holiday that falls on the first day of the month, the earliest possible date had to be observed in all years, as a precaution lest it be discovered at some point later in the day that the holiday had commenced at the preceding sundown, and that the day had become retroactively subject to Yom Tov restrictions.

The Talmud, in the tractate Rosh Hashanah (20b), cites an obscure regulation concerning the determining of the new month, to the effect that it could be declared only if the first sighting of the new moon appeared before noon on the twenty-ninth day of the month. Even the great Babylonian sage Samuel (who was also renowned as an astronomer) was at a loss to explain this cryptic tradition.

Some of our medieval sages took up the challenge of explaining the talmudic passage based on the advanced scientific knowledge of their age. The noted Spanish poet and philosopher Rabbi Judah Hallevi devoted a discussion to this topic in his famous theological treatise, the *Kuzari*.

Rabbi Judah began from the premise that the court may decree a new moon only if the day will last a full twenty-four hours. When the Talmud determines noon as the cut-off time, it is stating that until that hour it will be possible for somebody somewhere to the west of Jerusalem to fit in a full day of Rosh Hodesh.

Now let us try a few simple calculations. Keep in mind that according to Jewish law the day begins with nightfall on the previous day. Hence, assuming that nightfall comes at approximately 6 p.m., eighteen hours will have elapsed by the noon deadline in Jerusalem itself.

The choice of noon as the determining point presupposes that there is a place in the world where the day of Rosh Hodesh (or, to be precise, its preceding evening) had not yet commenced when it was noon in Jerusalem. The farthest westward point at which this would be true would thus, according to the Talmud, be eighteen hours west of Jerusalem, which is the equivalent of being six hours to the east of it. At this point, we will have entered a new day.

While conventional wisdom regarded such a location at the farthest extreme of Asia as the "land of the rising sun," whose clocks ran six hours earlier than Jerusalem, Rabbi Judah Hallevi insisted that all Sabbaths since the Creation had been set to commence in the Holy Land itself, and that the time in China is not six hours *earlier* than in Israel, but eighteen hours *later*:

> *A place must exist which is at the same time extreme west and the beginning of east. This is, for the Land of Israel, the beginning of the inhabited world, not only from the point of view of the Torah, but also from that of natural science. For it would be impossible for the days of the week to have the same names all over the world unless we fix one place which marks the beginning, and another one not far off… that one should be east absolute, and the other west absolute.*

What Rabbi Judah has established through this complex process of reasoning is the delineation of a Jewish version of the International Date Line! As noted, the location that is thereby designated is at a longitude six hours (or ninety degrees) east of Jerusalem. Since Jerusalem is situated at 35° longitude, this would place the halakhic date line at 125°.

Of course, throughout much of Jewish history these calculations were of no practical relevance. The line derived thereby runs through the farthest reaches of Siberia, China, and Japan, lands in which few self-respecting Jews were likely to have wandered.

With the modern Age of Discovery, this situation changed drastically. Not only did Jewish feet come to tread on the soils of Japan and Australia, but the world at large had established its own International Date Line at a conveniently uninhabited region in the Pacific Ocean, opposite the Greenwich median at 180° longitude. In theory, any Jews who might find themselves dispersed to those far-off domains between the two lines should be following a different calendar from their gentile neighbours.

In spite of the gradual blossoming of Jewish life in the Far East, the issue did not come up for serious discussion until 1941.

The event that sparked the debate was the flight of several hundred Eastern European yeshivah students, escaping the reign of Nazi terror, to the Far East. They were among several thousand desperate Jews whose lives were spared thanks to the heroism of Chiune Sugihara, the righteous Japanese consul in Kovno who disregarded the orders of his government and fought the Soviet insistence on the immediate closure of his consulate, so that he might issue as many visas as he physically could before the gates were fatally closed.

Following their arduous adventure on the Trans-Siberian Railroad, the meticulously observant students, mostly from the renowned Yeshivah of Mir, reached the

Japanese town of Kobe prior to being settled in Shanghai.

Kobe was situated between the Jewish and international date lines. In order to avoid transgressing the Sabbath, the yeshivah students initially kept it for two days each week, but eventually decided to resolve their doubts by telegraphing some of the foremost rabbinical authorities in Europe and Palestine.

The most prominent of the respondents was Rabbi Abraham Karelitz, the celebrated "*Hazon Ish*," who was firm in his commitment to Rabbi Judah Hallevi's version of the date line, insisting that the students observe their Sabbath on the day that the rest of the Japanese regarded as Sunday.

The seriousness with which these students regarded the matter became apparent later in 1941, when a group of them was given an opportunity to sail from Shanghai to Canada. Upon realizing that their ship would be crossing through the doubtful zone on Yom Kippur, requiring them to fast for two consecutive days, they decided to forego this rare chance at freedom. Before they could find another ship, the intensification of the war halted all traffic, and they remained precariously stranded in China until 1946.

The 125° longitude cuts right through the deserts of Western Australia, putting most of the continent on the "wrong" side of the halakhic date line. It would indeed follow from this that Australian Jews should always be one day out of sync from the rest of their society, keeping their Shabbat on Sunday.

However, there are some other halakhic opinions on the matter.

The most convenient of these is based on the argument from silence: The bulk of medieval rabbinic opinion simply ignores the issue altogether, and should therefore be counted as an overwhelming indication that the halakhah has no fixed doctrine about the placement of the date line. Individual communities should consequently be free to choose their own. This view found almost no support among the leading interpreters of Jewish religious law.

The *Hazon Ish* himself acknowledged, as had Rabbi Judah Hallevi, that the designated meridian need not be followed so precisely as to cut off small chunks of territory from the larger land masses. Accordingly, once we have established that the bulk of Asia lies to the east of the halakhic date line, those few extremities of Siberia or China that happen to cross the line can safely be treated as part of the larger land mass.

Unfortunately, this calculation would only serve to join the western third of Australia along with the rest of the country into the "wrong" side of the International Date Line.

A more effective halakhic solution is the alternative date line that has been posited by some rabbinic scholars at 145° west, which places Australia safely to its west. The defenders of this view point out that their line falls precisely halfway around the world from Jerusalem.

Though this option might elicit sighs of relief from the Jews of Sydney, Melbourne, or even Tokyo, it offers little solace to their unfortunate coreligionists in Hawaii, who have thereby been cut off from the familiar international calendar.

The stalwart Australian diaspora might yet have to ponder the possibilities of a two-day fast on Yom Kippur, or a third day of Rosh Hashanah.

Suggestions for Further Reading

Judah Hallevi. *The Kuzari (Kitab al Khazari); An Argument for the Faith of Israel.* Translated by Hartwig Hirschfeld. New York: Schocken Books, 1964.

Leitner, Y. *Operation Torah Rescue: The Escape of the Mirrer Yeshiva from War-Torn Poland to Shanghai, China.* Jerusalem: Feldheim, 1987.

Mochizuki, K., and D. Lee. *Passage to Freedom: The Sugihara Story.* New York: Lee & Low Books, 1997.

Pahmer, D. "The International Date Line and Related Issues." *Journal of Halacha and Contemporary Society* 21 (1991): 60-83.

Ta-Shma, Israel M. *Rabi Zerahyah ha-Levi ba'al ha-Ma'or u-vene hugo : le-toldot ha-sifrut ha-Rabanit bi-Provans.* Jerusalem: Mossad Harav Kook, 1992.

Vanity, Emptiness and the Throne of Glory*

The *'Aleinu* prayer, which is now recited at the conclusion of every Jewish prayer service, first appeared on the scene as part of the Additional Service for Rosh Hashanah. It is indeed a most appropriate text to introduce the theme of *Malkhuyyot*, the proclamation of God's sovereignty over the entire universe.

The unique tenor of the *'Aleinu*, full of confidence that idolatry and tyranny will imminently give way to universal acceptance of God's dominion by all the nations of the earth, distinguishes it from the majority of rabbinic prayers, which confined their scope to the Jewish nation.

The placement of the *'Aleinu* at the conclusion of all three daily prayer services was instituted because the medievals saw in it an expression of the highest ideals of Judaism.

The *'Aleinu's* triumphal tone led some medieval rabbis to ascribe it to Joshua, the conqueror of Israel. At any rate, the prevailing view among historical scholars sees

* *The Jewish Free Press*, Calgary, September 28, 2000, pp. 12–13.

it as the product of a time when the Temple was standing and a confident Jewish nation dwelled on its ancestral soil.

For later generations, it was more difficult to uphold their faith that humanity as a whole would come to acknowledge God's sovereignty. The change in attitude was occasioned largely by the conversion of the Roman Empire to Christianity in the fourth century. Hebrew liturgical poets who lived under the yoke of Byzantine oppression ceased hoping for a time when the world would voluntarily submit to God's will. Their works were filled instead with apocalyptic visions in which Israel and its messiah would prevail over their irreconcilable foes, especially the evil empire of Rome.

Like many other traditions that had their origins in ancient Palestine, the tendency to depict God's judgment on Rosh Hashanah as an ultimate confrontation between Israel and the heathen nations was continued by the early synagogue poets of medieval Germany. This motif came to pervade many of the familiar festival prayers in the Ashkenazic rite.

In light of these developments, we may readily understand how, though the *'Aleinu's* origins almost certainly predate the advent of Christianity, there was a widely held view in medieval Europe that it was a specifically anti-Christian text.

This accusation was directed primarily at the passage in the *'Aleinu* that speaks of heathens who "bow down to vanity and emptiness, and pray to a god who cannot save." The Hebrew word for "and emptiness"

– *varik* – has the same numerological value – *gimatria* – as "Yeshu," which was believed to be the Hebrew name of Jesus.

In spite of the historical anachronism implicit in this interpretation, it was taken very seriously by Christians and Jews alike. The influential Jewish mystical school of German Pietism (Hasidut Ashkenaz) set great store by numerological interpretations of the liturgy, and Rabbi Jacob Moelin (Maharil), the renowned authority on liturgical customs, was accustomed to spit when he pronounced *varik* (the word also sounds like the Hebrew word for spitting).

When the Christians heard, often through the agency of apostates, how the Jews construed the prayer, they were understandably offended, which led to the excising of the offending sentence from many prayer books, though it has been reintroduced, usually in brackets, into many recent printings.

Armed with a bit of arithmetical creativity, you can prove almost anything, and it did not take long for some clever individuals to find an anti-Islamic reference in the same sentence. The full phrase "to vanity and emptiness" adds up to the numerological sum of "Jesus and Mohamet." Unfortunately, the calculation requires some tampering with the spelling of the Muslim prophet's name (which should end with a *d*, not a *t*), as well as the adding of a letter to the Hebrew text, so that it reads *velarik* instead of *varik*. However, such is the power of a good *gimatria* that the "emended" spelling was introduced into several texts of the prayer book, and was solemnly discussed by the learned commentaries of the time.

For those who insisted on a correct spelling of Muhammad's name, an alternative *gimatria* was derived based on the end of the verse. The expression "to a god who cannot save" adds up to the desired sum, except that it also requires a tiny change in the Hebrew text, from "*el el lo yoshia*" to "*le'el lo yoshia*." While the emendation involves no change at all in the meaning of the Hebrew sentence, it happens that the original formulation was based on a biblical quotation, from Isaiah (45:20).

Some authorities, like Rabbi Judah the Pious, preferred a third version: "*el lo yoshia*" (to one who does not save), in order to remove the name of God entirely from this unsavoury setting.

It did not take long for our nimble numerologists to run into an unexpected problem. The consonantal text of *varik* forms an anagram of the word *yekaro*, which means that the two words share the same *gimatria*. *Yekaro* means "his glory," as in the clause "and the throne of his glory is in the heavens above."

Now, if they wanted to be consistent, then they would have to interpret this sentence as well as an allusion to Jesus, leading to implications that were far too ecumenical for any medieval Jew!

Though we might easily brush off this word game as a mere triviality, the medieval German rabbis treated it with the utmost seriousness, and several of the most distinguished halakhic authorities of the time voiced opinions on the question. In some prayer rites, the offending sentence was deleted or replaced by synonyms with different *gimatria* totals. An examination of the medieval Ashkenazic prayer books and commentaries reveals that much energy and ingenuity was being devoted to the quest for new ways to say "throne of glory" without forcing the innocent Jewish worshipper to inadvertently acknowledge the divinity of Jesus.

One of the obvious lessons to be derived from this story is that we should not build too much on the capricious game of *gimatria*. The whole episode reminds me of the excitement that surrounded the discovery a few years ago of mathematical codes in the Bible that supposedly proved beyond question its supernatural authorship and the authenticity of the Jewish oral tradition. All was well until the Christians began to apply the same methods, and were able to demonstrate equally irrefutable evidence that their own messiah was predicted in the numerical patterns of the Old Testament.

However, I think there is a more significant moral to be learned: namely, that our prayers should be more concerned with our own relationships with the Almighty, and less with passing judgment upon the followers of other faiths.

Suggestions for Further Reading

Elbaum, Yaaqov. "Concerning Two Textual Emendations in the *'Aleinu* Prayer," *Tarbiz* 42 (1972–73): 204–8.

Sperber, Daniel. *Minhage Yisra'el: Meqorot Ve-Toladot*, Jerusalem: Mosad ha-Rav Kuk, 1989–.

Wieder, Naphtali. "Regarding an Anti-Christian and Anti-Muslim *Gematria* (in the *'Alenu le-shabeah*" prayer)," *Sinai* 76 (1998):1–14.

Yahalom, Joseph *Poetry and Society in Jewish Galilee of Late Antiquity*, edited by M. Ayali, *Helal ben-Hayyim Library*, Tel Aviv: Hakibbutz Hameuchad, 1999 [Hebrew].

Sins in the Balance*

In a magazine article I happened to read recently, a Jewish actor spoke of how he envied his Christian friends for their convenient methods of obtaining forgiveness for their sins. A formal confession to the priest, the recitation of a specified number of Hail Marys – and the penitents can leave church with the assurance that the burden has been lifted from their shoulders. Jews lack such an automatic absolution process, and hence (according to the author of the quote) spend more of their time wrestling with unresolved guilt.

While this stereotypical generalization does not do justice to the nuances of either faith, and displays an abysmal ignorance of the atonement mechanisms associated with the Jewish High Holy Day season, I feel that it does point to an intriguing anomaly: In most areas of religious life it is Judaism that distinguishes itself, for better or for worse, by its concern for minute ritual detail, while the Christian tendency is towards sweeping generalization. However, when it comes the process of repentance,

* *Ha-Atid: Magazine of the Melbourne Hebrew Congregation,* Melbourne Australia, 4:4:16 (September-November 2000), pp. 11–12.

the dominant Jewish tradition takes a straightforward, pragmatic approach that focuses on identifying our shortcomings, renouncing them, and resolving not to repeat them in the future. On the other hand, classical Christian practice (as exemplified most strongly in the Roman Catholic church) has evolved elaborate rituals to absolve the penitents of their guilt.

In reality, Judaism has not been completely immune to the kinds of penitential rituals that we normally associate with Catholicism. Several ethical and halakhic works make reference to a Hebrew term known as "*teshuvat ha-mishkal*," which is best translated as "balance-penance." The basic premise of this concept is that transgressors should be required to undergo specific acts of punishment or suffering that are equivalent to the amounts of pleasure or profit that they enjoyed through their indiscretions.

Although such penitential regimens are mentioned occasionally in talmudic literature, they are treated as the extraordinary practices of saintly individuals, and not as norms to be followed by ordinary people. Their widespread adoption does not occur until the Middle Ages, in central Europe.

Ascetic practices were strongly encouraged by the *Hasidei Ashkenaz*, the pietistic sect that achieved far-reaching influence among the Jewish communities of twelfth- and thirteenth-century Germany. The *Book of the Pious*, the most important manifesto of the movement's ideals, commends a life of fasting and asceticism. Typical of its spiritual outlook is the story it recounts about a certain saint who was wont to spend the hottest days of summer lying among ants, and the winter days with his feet frozen into buckets of ice. When asked why such a righteous individual needed to resort to extreme acts of penance, he acknowledged that he was not personally guilty of such grave wrongdoing; however, he wished to alleviate the sufferings of the messiah. The tale concludes with the assurance that the saint eventually was assigned the most prestigious place in Paradise.

This account of radical self-abnegation, coupled with its concern for the pains of a suffering messiah, seems more appropriate to a Christian author than to one of the most distinguished Jewish teachers. Indeed, historians have observed that the penitential doctrines that prevailed among the Ashkenazic Jewish pietists were deeply imbued with the values of the surrounding Christian society. The notion that a penance should be commensurate with the sin is one that had been introduced around that time by the Franks; and detailed manuals were composed in order to guide the priests in assigning appropriate penances to their flocks.

A Jewish version of those penitential manuals was composed by Rabbi Eleazar Rokeah of Worms. Rabbi Eleazar had learned these disciplines from his teachers in the *Hasidei Ashkenaz* movement, but he insisted that they derived from an unbroken oral tradition going back to Moses at Sinai. It was in the Rokeah's classic formulation that the idea of "balance-penance" became the standard for subsequent Jewish writers. It was based on the assumption that each sin produces a spiritual imbalance that must be rectified.

Another class of penances was designed to ward off divine punishment in the next world by imposing a penalty that resembled the one that would have been inflicted by Torah law.

The catalogue of recommended torments included the aforementioned subjection to ice or insects, as well as the venerable practices of fasting, charity, and flagellation. Some sins call for abstaining from meat or wine, sleeping on boards, going unwashed for long periods of time, and the like.

The extremes to which people asked to be punished bordered on the pathological. Thus, for instance, the *Book of the Pious* dealt with the case of a person who asked his fellow to strike him to death. The rabbi ruled that it was permissible to strike him, but not to kill him.

A survey of the crimes for which penances had to be prescribed provides us with an index of the weaknesses to which our revered ancestors were prone. High on the list were sexual crimes, including adultery and indiscretions with Christian women and maidservants. The sources also discuss penances for murder and manslaughter. In such extreme cases, the criminal was ordered to forsake his home and assume the life of a wanderer. In each community that he visited he must confess his sin, submit himself to iron shackles, and allow himself to be trodden on by passersby on the synagogue doorstep.

The halakhic status of these penances underwent some interesting evolutions over the years. It appears they were originally intended to be administered by the pietist teachers whose role it was to hear the confessions and guide the sinners through their absolution. However, the communities were not comfortable with assigning such priest-like authority to Jewish sages, and instead accepted the regimens only on an individual basis, with the confessions being directed to the Almighty as part of the daily prayers, rather than to human intermediaries. This approach was adopted by Rabbi Eleazar Rokeah in his penitential manual. Nevertheless, we find that by the fifteenth century some Jewish towns were incorporating the penances into their communal regulations, using them as punishments for violations of public morals.

These extreme practices never caught on among Sepharadic Jews, whose typical attitude was more in keeping with Maimonides' derisive condemnation of people "who are not satisfied with what was forbidden by the Torah, but heap upon themselves additional prohibitions, including continual fasting that does them no good."

Even among the Ashkenazic authorities, there were several rabbis who voiced their reservations concerning the value of penitential practices. A particularly instructive example is contained in a responsum of Rabbi Ezekiel Landau (the *Noda' BiYhudah*). Upon being asked by his correspondent to recommend a regimen for a serious transgression (the individual in question had married the daughter of a woman with whom he had previously conducted a lengthy adulterous affair), the rabbi replied that he was unaccustomed to dealing with such matters since they have no basis in talmudic law. He declared that he normally avoided the kinds of moralistic tracts that recommend penitential regimens, and knew about them only from vague childhood memories.

In the end, Rabbi Landau acquiesced in prescribing a mild penance of fasting and philanthropy, but made it clear that such practices must always be seen as means towards contrition, and have no atoning power in themselves.

Rabbi Landau, like several other distinguished teachers (including Rabbi Shneur Zalman of Liady, Rabbi Moses Sofer, and more), was concerned that ascetic practices would come to be perceived as a quick substitute for the sincere and complete moral transformation that constitutes authentic Jewish repentance.

Suggestions for Further Reading

Baer, F. I. "The Religious-Social Tendency of 'Sefer Hasidim.'" *Zion* 3 (2) (1938):1–50.

Marcus, Ivan G. *Piety and Society: The Jewish Pietists of Medieval Germany*, edited by G. Vajda, *Études sur le Judaisme Médiéval*. Leiden: Brill, 1991.

Sperber, Daniel. *Minhage Yisra'el: Meqorot Ve-Toladot*. Jerusalem: Mosad ha-Rav Kuk, 1989–.

Zevin, Shelomoh Yosef. *The Festivals in Halachah: An Analysis of the Development of the Festival laws*, translated by M. Holder and Uri Kaploun, *ArtScroll Judaica classics*. New York and Jerusalem: Mesorah Publications and Hillel Press, 1999.

Atoning for Esau*

In our days, Yom Kippur is observed primarily as a day of fasting and synagogue prayer. In ancient times, however, what defined this holy day was the sequence of unique rituals that were performed by the High Priest in the Jerusalem Temple.

Among these rituals, surely one of the most awe-inspiring was that of the scapegoat. The High Priest would set aside two goats, and then cast lots to determine their fates. One of them was assigned "to the Lord" and sacrificed as a sin-offering. The other was designated "for Azazel." The priest confessed the transgressions of the entire people as he pressed his hands on this goat's head. Then the goat was sent away into the wilderness to perish, symbolically bearing with him the sins of Israel (Leviticus 16).

The sages of the Midrash examined every aspect of the scapegoat ritual in order to extract from it subtle lessons and symbols. One of their favourite methods was

* *The Jewish Free Press*, Calgary, September 13, 2001, pp. 22, 24.

to seek out thematic comparisons with similar images elsewhere in the Bible.

Basing themselves on a halakhic stipulation that the two goats that were subjected to the lottery must be identical in their appearance, size and value (*Yoma* 62a), some of the rabbis drew an analogy to those prototypical twins, Jacob and Esau. The former, the progenitor and representative of the Jewish nation, was set aside "for the Lord," whereas his demonic sibling, the symbolic ancestor of the wicked Roman Empire, was doomed to perish in a spiritual and eschatological wasteland. In the polarized universe of rabbinic preaching, Esau bore not only his own iniquities, but also those of Israel, who were thereby totally cleansed of all moral stains (*Genesis Rabbah* 65:9).

This kind of unrestrained vilification of Esau was standard fare in midrashic discourse, and reflected the frustrations felt by ancient Jews at the relentless triumphs of their evil occupier.

However, not all the rabbis were as willing to rejoice unconditionally at the downfall of their spiritual arch-enemy.

An extraordinary exposition of the scapegoat rite is found in a midrashic work known as *Seder Eliahu Zuta* (Chapter 19), a work whose dates and place of composition remain uncertain.

Seder Eliahu's interpretation seems at first to be identical to the one that we have been describing so far. The Midrash begins by developing the theme of how God will take away Jacob's sins and load them all upon Esau.

But the story does not end there.

In this version, Esau is permitted to plead his case before the Almighty: "Master of the universe, what strength do I possess, that you should heap upon me all of Jacob's sins?"

At this point, God is persuaded by the reasonableness of Esau's plea, and agrees to find a different destination for the unloading of Jacob's sins. Ultimately, God takes Israel's sins upon himself, causing the divine robes to be stained crimson.

This, says the *Seder Eliahu* midrash, is the significance of Isaiah's powerful prophecy (63:1–2), "Who is this that cometh from Edom, with dyed garments from Bozrah? ... Wherefore art thou red in thine apparel, and thy garments like him that treadeth in the wine-vat?"

Although Isaiah seems to be describing how God will exact bloody vengeance upon the despised Edom/Esau, our midrashic author has completely transformed the metaphor's significance. In the new version, God is actually showing compassion to Esau by retracting his original plan to burden him with Israel's sins and consenting to bear them upon himself.

In fact, the *Seder Eliahu* has added a new character to the allegorical drama. In addition to the two goats who symbolize Israel and Esau, we now have a third figure who ultimately assumes the sins of the other two. In order to fit this into the cast of biblical characters, the midrash attaches new importance to a figure who goes virtually unnoticed in the Torah's account.

According to the regulations set down in Leviticus 16:21, the scapegoat must be led into the wilderness "by the hand of a fit man." This individual has no apparent function in the story other than the technical one of making sure that the goat exits the Temple and makes it to its final, fatal destination.

However, in the *Seder Eliahu* the role of this obscure character has undergone a major redefinition. From a minor supporting part barely more important than a stagehand, he has been elevated to a starring role, as the representative of the Almighty himself! From an exegetical perspective, this interpretation helps clarify the Torah's enigmatic statement that the person who leads the scapegoat is required to wash his clothes after completing his mission. This makes sense if we presume that those clothes have been stained with the people's iniquities.

This midrashic shift in meaning would be remarkable if only for the uncharacteristic sympathy that it demonstrates towards the usually despised figure of Esau. However, from a theological perspective, it confronts us with even greater grounds for amazement: The representation of God, portrayed in human terms, taking upon himself the sins of Israel and the nations, is one that has familiar associations that we would not normally expect to find in a kosher Jewish discourse.

And in fact, we find that an interpretation on very similar lines was proposed by one of the most outstanding Christian homelists of antiquity, Origen of Caesarea. Origen identifies the figure who guides the scapegoat as

Jesus, who has allegorically donned "garments" of flesh and blood.

Now, Origen was both a neighbour and a contemporary of several of the foremost Jewish talmudic sages. From his base on the Israeli coast, he respected the Jews' mastery of the Hebrew scriptures, and his commentaries make frequent references to interpretations that he had learned from Jewish teachers. Modern Judaic scholarship has come to value Origen's writings as an important source of authentic midrashic traditions, some of which were not preserved in our standard compendia.

In most of the instances of similarity between Origen and the rabbis, it seems clear that the Church Father is borrowing from a prior Jewish tradition. However, in the present instance there are powerful reasons for suggesting that the borrowing might have been in the opposite direction.

We have already alluded to the strikingly Christian theology that is implied by the theme of God assuming human sins. To this we should add the unusually sympathetic consideration that is given to the image of Esau as the scapegoat. In almost every other presentation of Esau in midrashic literature, he is painted in the most negative of colours, a figure of unqualified moral and metaphysical depravity.

The universalistic outlook conveyed by the *Seder Eliahu Zuta* would have seemed astonishing if it were alluding to the pagan Roman Empire. The implications would be doubly astounding if we could date it after the fourth century C.E., after Constantine had converted the empire to Christianity and initiated a systemic persecution of Judaism.

In fact, a similar sentiment is expressed explicitly in the "sister" work known as *Seder Eliahu Rabbah Rabbah*. In explaining how a woman, Deborah, was able to rise to such a pre-eminent status as a judge and a prophet, the author of *Seder Eliyahu Rabbah* declares: "I call upon heaven and earth to witness: Whether Greek or Jew, whether male or female, whether slave or maidservant; In all cases, it is according to one's deeds that the holy spirit comes upon them."

Whether or not the midrashic preacher was conscious of the fact, his egalitarian affirmation was really a paraphrase of the words of St. Paul in his Epistle to the Galatians (3:28) in the New Testament.

The possibility therefore suggests itself that our uncommon midrashic exposition is offering us a glimpse into a different aspect of interfaith relations in the ancient world. Evidently, there were settings in which Jewish and Christian scholars dwelled together in a more open and relaxed atmosphere, treating one another with a measure of respect, and were occasionally ready to learn from each other.

Amicable social relationships may have allowed individuals to transcend their religious differences and to view the drama of divine forgiveness as a universal hope that is not restricted to a single nation or religion.

Suggestions for Further Reading

Halperin, David J. "Origen and Seder Eliyahu: A Meeting of Midrashic Trajectories?" In *Agendas for the Study of Midrash in the Twenty-First Century*, edited by Marc Lee Raphael, 18–41. Williamsburg, VA: Dept. of Religion College of William and Mary, 1999.

Hirshman, Marc G. *A Rivalry of Genius: Jewish and Christian Biblical Interpretation in Late Antiquity*. Translated by Batya Stein SUNY Series in Judaica. Albany: State University of New York Press, 1996.

Sukkot and Simhat Torah

Sukkot [the Feast of Tabernacles] is a biblical holiday celebrating the completion of the ingathering of the crops and the start of the rainy season, and commemorating the wanderings of the Israelites in the desert between the exodus from Egypt until their arrival in the promised land. It occurs in the autumn, and its main observances include (1) dwelling in a temporary structure known as a Sukkah during the course of the festival; (2) taking the "four species": a palm-branch [*lulav*], citron, myrtle and willow branches, which are carried and waved during the prayer service.

Following the seven days of Sukkot is a separate holiday called *Sh'mini Atzeret*: "the eight day of assembly."

The final day of the holiday, observed outside the Land of Israel as an extra day of Sh'mini Atzeret, was given a distinct identity in the Middle Ages as the "Rejoicing of the Law" [Simhat Torah], marking the conclusion of the annual cycle of reading the Torah, and the commencement of the new cycle.

Prince of Rain*

Sukkot marks the beginning of the rainy season according to the rhythms of the Middle Eastern climate. This transition is acknowledged in the liturgy by the fact that, from Sh'mini Atzeret until Passover, we include in the daily prayers a formula that praises God as the one "who causes the wind to blow and the rain to fall."

The season's first insertion of the phrase, during the Musaf service, is commemorated in the Ashkenazic rite with a special "*piyut*," a Hebrew liturgical poem devoted to the importance of rain and water. The *piyut* was composed by Rabbi Eleazar Hakalir, who was perhaps the foremost Hebrew liturgical poet of the classical age of that genre. A resident of the Land of Israel, probably during the seventh century, Rabbi Eleazar authored a formidable literary *oeuvre*, much of which has only recently been retrieved from manuscripts. Like most examples of the genre, his poems are distinguished by their extraordinary erudition, being full of obscure allusions to biblical and rabbinic passages.

* *The Jewish Free Press*, Calgary, September 23, 1999, pp. 8–9.

The opening words of his *piyut* for rain tend to jar the sensibilities of many modern readers. The cryptic Hebrew words translate roughly as follows: "Af B'ri is the name of the Prince of Rain who forms clouds and mists, which he empties and from which he pours water."

Many contemporary worshippers, brought up with the expectation that God should always be approached directly and not through intermediaries, are understandably taken aback by the poem's mythological tenor, which seems to divert our prayers to an obscure rain-god.

After all, Rabbi Yohanan stated in the Talmud that the key to rainfall is kept permanently in the custody of the Almighty and never lent out to agents (*Ta'anit* 2a). The medieval *Tosafot* commentary objected to this claim, noting the biblical account of how Elijah was given the power to bestow or withhold rain (1 Kings 17:1, 7). They resolved the apparent contradiction by observing that, though God might hand the proverbial keys to emissaries, those emissaries can never act on their own authority, but always in obedience to the divine command.

A different talmudic tradition declares that the rainfall in the Land of Israel is taken care of only by God himself; however, when it comes to other lands, he does appoint deputies.

In spite of attempts by Jewish rationalists to provide symbolic or allegorical interpretations for the offending texts, it is clear that our ancestors shared their world with diverse contingents of angels, demons, and other supernatural beings.

Who then is this mysterious Prince of Rains who is addressed in our *piyut*? The words *"af b'ri"* are taken from the book of Job (37:11), from a passage in which Job's companion Elihu tells how powerful storms provide evidence of God's dominion over creation. The passage is standardly translated into English as: "with moisture he saturates the thick clouds."

Like most of the Book of Job, the original Hebrew text here is inscrutable, and commentators have thrown up their hands in despair at deciphering it. The word *"af"* is generally assumed to be the common Hebrew particle signifying "furthermore" or "also." As for *"b'ri,"* it's anyone's guess. The King James translation cited above reads it as "with moisture." Other scholars connected it to words for "purity," "light" or "lightning." Hardly any of the commentators were persuaded to see an allusion to the name of an angel.

It is to be expected that the poet based his interpretation on a talmudic or midrashic source; however, his source has not come down to us.

Quite the contrary, an early guide to talmudic hermeneutics interprets the word *"af"* in its normal sense of "also," deducing from it that "the clouds and the rain are stubborn, and the Holy One must implore them to rain. And how do we know that just as he implores them to rain, so must he implore them to cease? From the word *'af'* meaning also."

Clearly, the author of this text did not understand *af* to be part of a proper name.

Nonetheless, Rabbi Eleazar Hakalir had an enthusiastic and reputable champion in the person of Rashi, whose commentary to Job states as follows: "Af B'ri is the name of an angel who presides over the clouds, and he distributes the Almighty's rains."

On one occasion in his commentary to the Talmud, Rashi found an additional pretext for squeezing in a reference to the Prince of Rains. This was in connection with a talmudic passage (*Ta'anit* 7b) that reads as follows:

> *Rain is withheld only on account of the sin of violence, as it states (Job 36:32): "He covereth his hands with the lightning." This implies that for the sin of 'their hands' [i.e., violence] he covers the light....*
>
> *And 'light' means nothing other than rain, as it states: 'He spreadeth abroad the cloud of his lightning.'"*

This last-mentioned quotation is the continuation of the "*af b'ri*" verse in Job, and Rashi takes that fact into account when he observes (unnecessarily, it seems) that "the angel named Af B'ri will scatter the cloud of his light, namely his rain."

Rashi's insistence that Af B'ri is the angel in charge of rain involves him in an additional difficulty, since the Talmud elsewhere makes reference to a *different* rain-angel, as we find in the following passage (*Yoma* 20b–21a):

> *Our Rabbis taught: There are three sounds that extend from one end of the world to the other; and they*

are: the sound of the sun, the sound of the throngs of Rome, and the sound of a soul as it leaves the body. ... Some add: the sound of "Ridia."

In explaining the word "*Ridia*" Rashi states that "it is the angel in charge of watering the earth with rain from the heavens above and from the deep waters below."

A medieval Babylonian *Ga'on* reported that in his days it was still possible to hear harsh voices emerging from beneath lakes and pools. The people, Jews and Arabs alike, ascribed those voices to Ridia.

Rashi's explanation is based on an interpretation by the Babylonian talmudic sage Rabbah (*Ta'anit* 25b). Commenting on the words of the Psalmist (42:8), "Deep calleth unto deep at the voice of thy cataracts," Rabbah reported, "I myself have seen Ridia, and he resembles a three-year-old heifer with its lips split. To the upper deep he says 'Restrain your waters.' To the lower deep he says 'Let your waters burst forth' ...."

As Angels of Rain go, this heifer-like Ridia is indeed an imposing creature. Some scholars have speculated that Ridia is a Judaized version of the Persian angel-goddess Aredvi Sura, who was believed to preside over the celestial waters, which were a source of fertility as well as immortality.

When all is said and done, whether we prefer to address our prayers directly to the Almighty, or to convey them via a prince or angel, I am sure that we all join in hoping for moisture and abundance for Israel and the world.

Suggestions for Further Reading

Corbin, Henry. *Spiritual Body and Celestial Earth, Bollingen Series*, Princeton: Princeton University Press, 1977.

Feldman, Moses J. *Areshet Sefatenu: Source Book of Hebrew Prayer and Proverb*, 4 vols., St. Louis, 1942 [Hebrew].

Goldschmidt, Daniel, ed. *Mahzor Sukkot Li-Shmini 'Atzeret ve-Simhat Torah*, Jerusalem: Koren, 1981.

Harkavy, Alexander. *Hadashim Gam Yeshanim*, Jerusalem: Karmi'el, 1970.

Kohut, Alexander. *Aruch Completum*, 8 vols., Vienna-New York [Hebrew].

———. *Supplement to 'Aruch Completum*, Jerusalem: Makor, 1970 [Hebrew].

Margaliot, Reuben. Mal'akhé 'Elyon, Jerusalem: Mosad Harav Kook, 1964.

Come Gather 'Round, People*

Among the holidays of the Hebrew calendar, Sukkot has been endowed with more than its share of rituals and ceremonies. We are familiar with its rustic booths, the lulav and etrog, and with the solemn *Hoshana* processions around the synagogue.

There is, however, a momentous biblical precept associated with Sukkot that has been largely forgotten. This ceremony, known as the *Hak-hel* ["gather together"], is described in the Book of Deuteronomy 31:12:

> *At the end of seven years, in the solemnity of the year of release, in the feast of tabernacles. When all Israel is come to appear before the Lord thy God in the place which he shall choose, thou shalt read this law before all Israel in their hearing. Gather the people together, men, and women, and children, and thy stranger that is within thy gates, that they may hear, and that they may learn, and fear the Lord your God, and observe to do all the words of this law.*

* *The Jewish Free Press*, Calgary, October 19, 2000, pp. 22–23.

Though the Torah seems to be ordaining the ceremony for the septennial Sabbatical year, the Jewish oral tradition understood that it was to take place at the beginning of the eighth year, that is to say, in the year following the sabbatical.

As for the date upon which the *Hak-hel* should be convened, rabbinic sources confront us with an array of contradictory and confusing traditions about which of the eight days of Sukkot the Torah had in mind. The Babylonian Talmud (*Sotah* 41a–b) understood that it should be on the second day (that is, the first day of *Hol ha-Mo'ed*), and this interpretation has been accepted as normative. However, according to accurate manuscripts of the Mishnah, the ceremony actually took place after the completion of the festival, on the night following *Sh'mini Atzeret* or of the following day, when the full complement of pilgrims were assembled in Jerusalem and had not yet begun their homeward journeys. The gathering was attended by men, women, and children alike.

The prevailing tradition declared that it was the king who should read the Torah to the people, and tells of one such ceremony in which King Agrippa did the reading. A special platform was constructed for the occasion and trumpets were sounded. The pageantry was heightened as the Torah scroll was passed around among the various Temple officials until the High Priest handed it to the monarch. On this occasion, Agrippa was so moved by the scriptural reading that he began to weep and to question his own right to the throne of Israel, since he was descended from the Herodian line of Idumean converts. The people cried out, "Do not fear, Agrippa! You are our brother, you are our brother."

It would be reasonable to expect that the practice of *Hak-hel* would cease with the loss of Jewish sovereignty and the destruction of Jerusalem. And yet we find that aspects of the *Hak-hel* continued to be observed even while the Temple lay in ruins. Thus, there is evidence that it was carried out in the academy of Yavneh, the main centre of Jewish spiritual leadership in the generation following the fall of Jerusalem. The rabbis of the time transferred to their own institutions, such as the courts, synagogues, and academies, several of the functions that had hitherto been the prerogatives of the Temple and its priesthood.

It is probable that the ideal of the *Hak-hel* also played a crucial role in shaping the rhythms of the Torah reading in the Land of Israel.

It has long been recognized that the Jews in the Holy Land, during the talmudic and early medieval eras, divided the weekly readings from the Torah according to the "triennial cycle." In actuality, the complete reading of the Torah was completed over a span of three and one half years. Recent scholarship has argued persuasively that this system was designed so that two cycles could be completed in exactly seven years. It was at the conclusion of this double cycle that a "*Simhat Torah*" would be celebrated on the date that coincided with the biblical *Hak-hel* gathering. When the Babylonian Jews introduced their own one-year Torah-reading cycle, they also arranged it so that it would conclude and recommence at the end of Sukkot, the date on which we still celebrate *Simhat Torah*.

Even during the Middle Ages, the *Hak-hel* did not cease. The observance of a *Hak-hel* ceremony with great pomp and ceremony was attested as late as the eleventh century. At this time, the Jewish presence in Jerusalem was enjoying a revival such as it had not known since the days of the Second Temple, and the holy city again played host to the great rabbinical academy of the Land of Israel.

When the Muslims liberated Jerusalem from the Byzantine Christians, the Jewish community was quick to purchase rights to the Mount of Olives. The biblical character of Sukkot as a time of pilgrimage was reinstated, as Jews from around the world flocked to their capital, a development that helped fortify the ties between Israel and the diaspora communities.

Documents from this time describe a solemn gathering that was convened on the Mount of Olives at the end of Sukkot. To the accompaniment of song, the pilgrims would march around the gates of Jerusalem and then proceed to the Mount of Olives for prayer. The occasion was also used to issue official proclamations regarding rabbinical appointments, the religious calendar (at a time when Palestinian Jewry was reclaiming its ancient prerogative over the determining of the sacred calendar) and other matters of public interest. Elaborate prayers were recited for the welfare of the academy's benefactors, even as grave maledictions were directed at the Karaite heretics. The imposing proportions of the event were not lost on Christian and Muslim chroniclers, who describe it with great interest.

It is difficult not to be amazed by the sheer tenacity of this ancient rite, and by our ancestors' determination to keep it alive for so long after the destruction of the Temple. Though there are many possible reasons for the phenomenon, I feel that much of the *Hak-hel* gathering's attraction stemmed from the way in which it gave tangible expression to that most evasive of ideals: the unity of the Jewish people.

Suggestions for Further Reading

Gil, Moshe. *Palestine during the First Muslim Period (634–1099)*, edited by S. Simonsohn, Vol. 1, *Publications of the Diaspora Research Institute.* Tel-Aviv: Tel-Aviv University Press and the Ministry of Defense Publishing House, 1983 [Hebrew].

Henshke, David. "When is the Time of *Hak-hel*?", *Tarbiz* 61(2) (1992): 177–94.

Naeh, Shlomoh. "The Torah Reading Cycle in Early Palestine: A Re-Examination," *Tarbiz* 67(2) (1998):167–87.

Zevin, S. Z., ed. *Talmudic Encyclopedia*, Jerusalem: Talmudic Encyclopedia Institute, 1961– [Hebrew].

The Mysterious Origins of Simhat Torah*

Nobody would question the appropriateness of holding a joyous celebration for the conclusion of the annual Torah-reading cycle. Even according to the ancient rite of the Land of Israel, where the Torah was chanted over a period of three and a half years, and did not conclude at a specific season of the year, a "Simhat Torah" ceremony was often held to mark that occasion.

What is much less obvious is how Simhat Torah came to be observed on its current date, on the "extra" day that is appended to Sh'mini 'Atzeret, at the culmination of the Sukkot season. Neither Sukkot nor Sh'mini 'Atzeret, whether viewed as agricultural or historical holidays, has any special relevance to the theme of Torah. Quite the contrary: There are several alternative dates in our sacred calendar that would be much more suitable for finishing and recommencing the reading of the Torah. Two alternatives that spring readily to mind are Shavu'ot, which commemorates the giving of the Torah at Sinai, and Rosh Hashanah, celebrated as the start of the new year.

* *The Jewish Free Press*, Calgary. October 10, 1998, pp. 10–11.

As we trace the obscure origins of Simhat Torah, we note that there has not always been clear agreement about when it should be observed. Several medieval Spanish authorities record a custom, ascribed to the Babylonian *Ge'onim,* of reading the first verses of the Torah (though not necessarily from an official scroll) on the afternoon of Yom Kippur. They cite as their reason the following legend:

> *Throughout the Ten Days of Repentance, Satan has been accusing Israel, arguing "Behold, the Torah which you have bestowed upon Israel – they have already done with it!"*
>
> *Now, when the Holy One hears them beginning again from Genesis, he immediately rebukes Satan saying "Look how, as soon as they complete it, they immediately start over again, so great is their love for my Torah!"*

It stands to reason, if the new cycle was begun on Yom Kippur, then the old one must have been concluded, with the reading of the final section of Deuteronomy, slightly before that. However, the sources are unclear about the exact date.

A more direct thematic link between the Day of Atonement and Simhat Torah is implied by the traditional Jewish chronology, according to which it was on Yom Kippur that the Almighty yielded to Moses' entreaties to forgive Israel for worshipping the golden calf, and consented to give Israel the second tablets of the law.

With such powerful reasons for observing Simhat Torah on Yom Kippur, it is all the more difficult to justify how it came to be celebrated on its current date on the second day of Sh'mini 'Atzeret.

One factor that might have influenced the choice was a talmudic tradition that designates Deuteronomy 28, with its fire-and-brimstone threats against those who disobey God, as the fitting scriptural reading for the Sabbath preceding Rosh Hashanah, the Day of Judgment, "so that the year and all its curses will be put behind us" (*Megillah* 31b). Following the normal divisions of the reading into weekly *parshiyot*, this would result in the reading of the entire Torah being completed just after the current date of Simhat Torah.

A more decisive reason for the choice of date had to do with its Prophetic reading (haftarah). According to the rules set out in the Talmud (*Megillah* 31a), the correct haftarah for the second day of Sh'mini 'Atzeret is 1 Kings 8, which relates how King Solomon blessed the people at the dedication of the newly erected Temple, an event that is usually understood to have occurred on the eighth day of Sukkot – that is to say, on Sh'mini 'Atzeret.

The readings from the Torah and the Prophets ought normally to share elements in common, and indeed Solomon's blessings bear a thematic affinity to the ones recited by the dying Moses in the closing verses of the Torah, making that day an appropriate one on which to conclude the annual Torah-reading cycle.

At this point, readers who are familiar with the holiday liturgy will undoubtedly be objecting: What is all this talk about a reading from the Book of Kings? Everybody knows that the haftarah for Simhat Torah is the opening of the Book of Joshua, which is the direct continuation of the end of Deuteronomy, but has no connection at all to Sh'mini 'Atzeret!

The truth is that, though Joshua Chapter 1 is now the universally accepted haftarah for Simhat Torah, this has not always been the case. Early sources inform us that its acceptance as haftarah was achieved only after a prolonged struggle, seeing that it contradicts the explicit injunctions of the Talmud.

During the early medieval era, communities throughout the Jewish world wavered about whether they should retain the old talmudic haftarah about Solomon's Sukkot blessings, or adopt the new one describing God's exhortations to Joshua. Various localities preferred the one, or the other, or followed some combination of both texts.

A few scholars dismissed the new custom as nothing more than a flagrant mistake, while others tried to justify it by noting that the selection of a haftarah is a matter of recommended custom rather than actual law, and that this particular innovation could be ascribed to the authority of the earliest post-talmudic teachers of Babylonia. At any rate, they noted, there is a talmudic principle that "custom can override the halakhah."

Eventually the original talmudic haftarah from the Book of Kings was completely pushed aside and virtually forgotten.

When that happened, we lost a vital clue to the obscure beginnings of Simhat Torah.

Suggestions for Further Reading

Yaari, A. *Toledot Hag Simhat Torah*, Jerusalem: Moṣad Harav Kook, 1989.

Hanukkah

Hanukkah [Dedication] is an eight-day holiday commemorating the successful insurrection by Jewish traditionalists against the religious persecutions of the Hellenistic Greeks and their collaborators in the early second century B.C.E. The festival occurs in midwinter, and its principal ritual is the lighting of lamps.

Getting a Handel on Hanukkah*

Unlike episodes from Jewish sacred history that were familiar to Christians because of their inclusion in the Bible, the Hanukkah story has left few traces in the artistic traditions of Western civilization.

A notable exception is G. F. Handel's oratorio "Judas Maccabeus," which celebrates the victories of the ancient Jewish loyalists against their pagan foes. That grand work continues to enjoy enormous popularity over the years, and one of its themes, "See the Conquering Hero Comes," has been adopted by Jews as a veritable Hanukkah melody; though, if the truth be told, it did not appear in the original version of "Judas Maccabeus," but was grafted subsequently from Handel's later oratorio about Joshua.

That Handel and his audience should be familiar with the exploits of Judah Maccabee need not surprise us, since the Books of Maccabees were included in the Apocrypha, the additions to the ancient Greek Bible translations that were in use among ancient Egyptian

* *The Jewish Free Press*, Calgary, December 10, 1998, p. 24.

Jews, but which were ultimately excluded from the official Hebrew canon. The Apocrypha were still in widespread circulation among Christians in Handel's time, as were the historical chronicles of Josephus Flavius, who provided a detailed history of the Maccabean uprising.

Nevertheless, it is not immediately apparent why crowds of gentile concert-goers should have been interested in an ancient Jewish struggle for religious liberty.

The answer to this question requires some knowledge of the events that were taking place in Britain at the time when Handel was composing "Judas Maccabeus."

Supporters of the deposed dynasty of King James had recently mounted their final and most serious attempt to regain the throne. Charles Edward Stuart, the "Young Pretender," had recently returned to Scotland from his French exile and had gathered around himself an army of Scottish highlanders, determined to recapture the throne from Handel's patron George II, whose German-born father had brought him to England from the old country.

In 1745, "Bonnie Prince Charlie" began a victorious campaign from Scotland through to England, and his forces seemed unstoppable. For a while it appeared as if London and the English heartland would fall to the Stuart forces. The tide was turned in April 1746, when the Duke of Cumberland routed the Jacobite armies in the ruthless massacre at Culloden Moor.

The bitter civil war called for inspiring patriotic music, an art at which Handel excelled. While he may have had little enthusiasm for the ancient Jewish successes over Antiochus Epiphanes, Handel saw in that exploit a fitting paradigm for England's recent deliverance from a grave threat.

The oratorio's tone of pompous nationalism would bring it enduring appeal in Germany; though under the Nazi regime, not surprisingly, its title character had to be camouflaged as "Wilhelm von Nassau."

For all its success, there are few critics who would rank the magisterial strains of Judas Maccabeus among Handel's finest works. In actuality, the composer himself openly shared that negative assessment.

He had recently introduced some changes to his method of financing his projects. Initially, Handel had sold subscriptions, which required the subscribers to commit themselves to several performances, a system that allowed him considerable independence in maintaining artistic standards.

Recently, however, the diminishing popularity of his operatic productions had impelled him to market his wares more directly. Now, if he were to be financially successful, he would have to cater more flagrantly to the lower aesthetic standards of popular tastes, a fact that is very much in evidence in "Judas Maccabeus."

The hasty quality of this oratorio is evident from the German-born composer's bloopers, stemming from misunderstandings of some of the more difficult English words in the libretto, which he could not be bothered to look up in the dictionary.

Although he did not compose "Judas Maccabeus" for a Jewish audience, nor with any thought of the

Hanukkah festival, the oratorio achieved immediate popularity among England's small Jewish community, which totalled no more than seven thousand souls at that time. In spite of their paltry numbers, Handel recognized that Jewish patrons of the arts made up a substantial proportion of its audience. This phenomenon inspired Handel to compose a series of additional oratorios devoted to Jewish heroes, including Solomon, Joshua, Susanna, and Jephtha.

Thus, though Handel might originally have envisaged Judah Maccabee as a pageant of English patriotism, rather than as a source of Jewish national pride, in some ways "Judas Maccabeus" can justifiably be considered a work of Jewish art.

Suggestions for Further Reading

Dean, W. *Handel's Dramatic Oratorios and Masques.* New York: Oxford University Press, 1959.

Hogwood, C., and A. Hicks. *Handel.* London: Thames and Hudson, 1984.

Lipman, V. "England." In *Jewish Art and Civilization*, edited by G. Wigoder, New York: Walker, 1972.

Young, P. M. *The Oratorios of Handel.* London: D. Dobson, 1949.

Burning Issue*

The precept of lighting candles on Hanukkah is intended to bear public testimony to the great miracles of the defeat of the Hellenistic forces and the rededication of the Temple. For this reason, the Talmud requires that the Hanukkah lamps be stationed outside the doorway, or on a second-storey window that opens onto the street, allowing them to be observed by passersby (*Shabbat* 22a).

In talmudic times, indoor lighting of Hanukkah lights was an exceptional occurrence, a special dispensation that was allowed by the rabbis of the time on account of flare-ups of Zoroastrian religious persecution.

During the Middle Ages, when Jewish communities flourished in many parts of Europe, we discover to our surprise that indoor candle-lighting had become the almost universal norm, and nobody was observing the original talmudic tradition of placing their menorahs outside the house.

* *The Jewish Free Press*, Calgary, December 2, 1999, p. 20.

The rabbis of the time were keenly aware of the discrepancy, but were not certain how to account for it. The most widely quoted rationale posited that the talmudic sages, in order to escape the perils of Zoroastrian persecution in their own generation, had issued a decree that candles be lit indoors; and for some reason had never gotten around to revoking it. Since then, even though the grounds for the edict had long ceased to exist, no subsequent court possessed the authority to repeal it.

A few authorities have suggested a more prosaic reason for the change. A very compelling factor that discouraged outdoor Hanukkah lighting was the weather. Strong winds and torrential rains occurred more frequently in the northern European climes than in the Middle Eastern lands where the rules had originally been formulated. This made it a daunting challenge to keep the flames lit without resorting to complex and costly equipment, such as glass cases for the candles.

Interestingly, none of the medieval sources that deal with this question contain the remotest suggestion that Hanukkah was considered offensive to the religious sensibilities of Christian neighbours. The phenomenon of Jews having to conceal their candles from hostile gentiles is invariably presented as a scenario from the distant past.

It therefore comes as something of a surprise to read the words of the prominent fourteenth-century Spanish halakhist Rabbi Jeroham ben Meshullam, who wrote that "some people are accustomed to lighting it inside the doorway that opens to the courtyard, because gentiles and thieves are common."

Rabbi Jeroham's misgivings might simply be motivated by the prospect of stolen menorahs, but what are we to do about the puzzling ruling by the fifteenth-century Rabbi Joseph ben Moses, who wrote that "In a house belonging to a non-Jew, a person should light only one candle and one shammash. Even though the non-Jew would not object to two or three candles, there is always that one case in a hundred when it could lead to danger, and it would bring discredit upon the precept."

Since Rabbi Joseph states explicitly that the gentile in question has no problem in principle with his Jewish tenant lighting candles, what difference does it make how many candles he lights?

I suspect that the issue here is not a theological principle, but an eminently practical one. Medieval Jews had acquired some notoriety for causing accidental conflagrations with their Sabbath candles. According to talmudic halakhah, it is permitted to extinguish a fire on Shabbat only in order to save lives, but not to prevent destruction of property. Therefore, when fires did break out in their homes and neighbourhoods on Friday nights or Saturdays, Jews were reluctant to extinguish them, and the flames could spread rapidly through their ramshackle neighbourhoods and beyond.

It is understandable that otherwise well-disposed Christian landlords could become very apprehensive at the prospect of eight days of Jewish candle-lighting.

Through their scrupulous adherence to the Sabbath prohibitions, Jews had occasionally placed themselves in danger of injury at the hands of enraged Christians who blamed them for promoting large-scale conflagrations, and vented their wrath in the form of bloody pogroms.

It was these kinds of considerations that led many influential medieval rabbis to relax the restrictions on putting out fires on Sabbath. Several French and German authorities allude to cases where the irate gentiles, on determining that the fire had originated from a Jewish home, would cast the Jews into the flames.

Under the circumstances, it is not surprising that Rabbi Joseph ben Moses was willing to cut down on the number of Hanukkah candles in order to allay the fears of a Christian landlord.

And I think that we can all take this as a valuable reminder to take appropriate precautions in preparing our holiday candles, so as not to bring discredit or calamity upon this joyous precept.

Suggestions for Further Reading

Sperber, Daniel. *Minhage Yisra'el: Meqorot Ve-Toladot.* Jerusalem: Mosad ha-Rav Kuk, 1989–.

The Wicked Hasmonean Priest*

We have all learned to admire them as supreme Jewish heroes: The five sons of Mattathias the Hasmonean, the freedom fighters whose heroic exploits against religious persecution brought about the celebration of Hanukkah.

The leader of the revolt, Judah Maccabee, was the first of the brothers to fall in battle before the goals of the rebellion had been accomplished. It was left to his brother Jonathan to complete the job, removing the last Greek garrison from the city of Jerusalem and initiating a century of Jewish independence. Jonathan assumed the High Priesthood, beginning an unbroken line of Hasmonean High Priests that continued from 163 B.C.E. until 37 B.C.E.

And yet, to judge from contemporary documents, many Jews were less than appreciative of this Hanukkah hero, and saw him as an enemy of Judaism and the Jewish people.

---

* *The Jewish Free Press*, Calgary, December 21, 2000, pp. 24–25.

This hostility is most evident in an ancient commentary to the Book of Habakkuk that was included among the Dead Sea Scrolls at Qumran. The work in question belongs to a special genre known as *Pesher*, in which the words of the biblical prophets were applied to events in recent history.

The Habakkuk Pesher has a great deal to say about a figure whom it dubs the "Wicked Priest." This villainous character, according to the author,

> *was called in the name of truth when he first arose. But when he ruled over Israel his heart became proud, and he forsook God and betrayed the precepts for the sake of riches.*

The Pesher accuses the Wicked Priest of corruption and oppressing the poor, and of generally violating God's law. He profaned the holy city of Jerusalem and its Temple with terrible abominations.

But the gravest of his crimes was his persecution of the person known as the "Teacher of Righteousness." As described in the Qumran scrolls, this figure was a revered individual, endowed with unique spiritual wisdom and revelation, who instructed his devoted disciples in the true meaning of the Torah.

The author of the Habakkuk Pesher relates that the Wicked Priest became arrogant in his power, leading him to violate God's laws and to cause unspecified suffering to the Teacher and his followers.

Ultimately the Wicked Priest met his deserved retribution. He fell into the hands of enemies who inflicted bitter suffering upon him.

Who were the Wicked Priest and the Teacher of Righteousness? These questions are crucial to any proper evaluation of the Dead Sea Scrolls and their message.

The history of the Second Jewish Commonwealth provides us with a number of candidates for the role of Wicked Priest. Several figures of priestly lineage were counted among the leading proponents of the Hellenistic reforms that sparked the Maccabean uprising.

Thus, for example, an individual named Jason (originally Joshua), scion of an aristocratic priestly family, purchased the High Priesthood from Antiochus Epiphanes, and used his three-year term of office to institute pagan practices in Judea. He was eventually deposed, and ended his days as a rootless exile who perished miserably at Sparta.

His rival and successor, Menelaus (known previously by his Hebrew name Honio or Onias), was even more resolute in his campaign against Judaism. A virtual civil war erupted during his reign, until Antiochus determined that the only way to restore peace among the rival factions was by deposing Menelaus and exiling him to the Syrian town of Berea, where he was put to death in his tenth year of office.

The next infamous figure in the series was Alcimus, a stubborn and ruthless opponent of the Hasmoneans who served as High Priest under the pro-Greek regime and came to a sordid end, stricken with a painful and debilitating paralysis.

Although some of the details mentioned in the Habakkuk Pesher – such as the allusion to the priest's righteous beginnings – remain unexplained by the known facts of these priests' biographies, it is not entirely inconceivable that one of these wretched figures could have been the Wicked Priest.

However, a virtual consensus has developed among interpreters of the Dead Sea Scrolls that the most likely identity for the Wicked Priest of the Habakkuk Pesher was the Hasmonean ruler Jonathan, the brother of Judah Maccabee. Almost all the expressions in the document, after we have made allowances for their flowery and cryptic style, can be readily linked to known episodes in Jonathan's life.

Jonathan's initial appearance on the stage of history, as a champion of traditional Judaism against pagan reforms and Seleucid oppression, was applauded by loyal Jews. However, once the revolt had elevated him to a position of leadership, his activities began to provoke criticism from many circles.

We know from other sources that Jonathan's most harshly condemned act was when he appointed himself High Priest, an office that had previously been the exclusive birthright of the ancient dynasty of the Zadokites. It is probable that the origin of the Sadducee sect is to be traced to this event. Some contemporaries, who might otherwise have tolerated Jonathan's High Priestly status, were nevertheless dismayed that he and his successors laid claim to the monarchy as well. The concentration of so much authority in the hands of a single individual was exceptional in Jewish history.

The Habakkuk Pesher's description of the Wicked Priest's dreadful demise also dovetails nicely with the known facts of Jonathan's life. The Hasmonean ruler met an ignominious end when he was treacherously imprisoned by the Syrian general Tryphon, who kept him in a dungeon until his execution. In the eyes of the Habakkuk Pesher's author, this pathetic end of a heroic Jewish freedom fighter was a just settling of accounts.

The one detail in this account that remains obscure is the dispute that arose between Jonathan and the Teacher of Righteousness. The Second Temple era was replete with sectarian controversies over the correct interpretation of the Torah, but our sources do not yet allow us to identify with any degree of certainty the specific issue that brought about the schism between the Wicked Priest and the Teacher of Righteousness, a schism that may have led to the founding of the Essene community by the shores of the Dead Sea.

If this theory is correct, then Jonathan the Hasmonean can join the ranks of many other war heroes and liberators who found it easier to rally their followers against a common enemy than to maintain their loyalty amid the obstacles of day-to-day politics.

Suggestions for Further Reading

Avi-Yonah, Michael, and Zvi Baras, eds. *Society and Religion in the Second Temple Period*, World History of the Jewish People: First Series: Ancient Time, Jerusalem: Massada Publishing, 1977.

Vermès, Géza. *Discovery in the Judean Desert*, New York: Desclee, 1956.

———. The Complete Dead Sea Scrolls in English, London: Penguin, 1995.

A Megillah for Hanukkah*

Although Hanukkah was established in order to commemorate a momentous exploit in Jewish history, the traditional documents of Jewish religious literature do not really say much about the historical events that are being celebrated.

The Maccabean revolt occurred too late to be recorded in the Bible; and the Talmud and Midrash speak only in vague terms of the Hasmonean triumph over the Greeks, the purification of the Temple, some cases of martyrdom, and the famous miracle of the oil cruse.

Arguably, it is possible to be an observant and knowledgeable Jew without having any familiarity with the major battles or heroes of the Maccabean revolt.

For many Jewish communities during the Middle Ages, this deficiency was offset by the availability of an account of the Hanukkah story that usually circulated under the name "the Scroll of Antiochus," though it was also known by such diverse titles as "the Scroll of the Hasmoneans," "the Scroll of the Greeks," or "the Scroll

* *The Jewish Free Press*, Calgary, November 22, 2001, pp. 8–9.

of Hanukkah." The best-known text was in Aramaic, but Hebrew and Arabic versions were also in existence.

There is no consensus about when the Scroll of Antiochus was composed. The most extreme claim for its antiquity was that of the tenth-century teacher Sa'adia Ga'on, who claimed that the scroll had been written down close to the time of the events that it recounts; i.e., in the middle of the second century B.C.E. An eighth-century compendium of Jewish law known as *Halakhot Gedolot* ascribed the work to the elders of the Houses of Shammai and Hillel, sometime in the first century C.E.; however, this claim is not found in all the manuscripts of *Halakhot Gedolot*. An analysis of the scroll's Aramaic dialect seems to point to the talmudic era (2nd–5th centuries), but this phenomenon has been explained away as an instance of the author's successfully imitating the style of earlier texts.

In the absence of clear-cut evidence for the scroll's ancient origins, most historians have taken a cautious position, dating it to the early medieval era, close to the rise of the Arab empire.

In order to explain why it should have been composed at this particular time, several scholars tried to draw conclusions from Sa'adia Ga'on's attitude towards it.

Sa'adia was renowned as an aggressive champion of the rabbinic oral tradition, a tradition that was being challenged in his time by the Karaites, a Jewish movement that rejected the Talmud and relied exclusively on the authority of the Bible.

Hanukkah, a holiday with no biblical source, was a convenient target for the Karaite polemical assaults on rabbinic tradition. It was in response to such charges that Sa'adia was impelled to make exaggerated claims about the scroll's antiquity and authority.

In addition to the above-mentioned assertion about its early date, Sa'adia found other ways in which to treat the scroll as if it were a full-fledged biblical book, with a status similar to that of Esther. In one of his commentaries, he cites a proof-text from the Scroll of Antiochus as if it were a biblical verse. He also mentions that it was customary to copy the scroll with vowels and cantillation signs, and to divide it into *parshiyot*, practices that were rarely applied to texts outside the biblical canon. Sa'adia even composed an Arabic translation to it, complete with a learned preface, just as he did for the books of the Bible.

Sa'adia's efforts on behalf of the Scroll of Antiochus led to its widespread acceptance by many Jewish communities, including those of Spain, Italy, Yemen, and Persia. Its text was included in many manuscripts and early printed editions of the Bible, as well as in prayer books. Several medieval rabbis report that the Scroll was read publicly as part of the Hanukkah services, usually on the Sabbath that occurred during the holiday.

Differing customs existed as to when the scroll should be chanted in the synagogue: Some localities did so prior to the Haftarah on the Saturday morning of Hanukkah, or immediately following it; others read it late in the afternoon, at the end of the Minhah service. Arabic-speaking Jewish communities normally recited it to the accompaniment of Sa'adia's Arabic translation.

The Italian Rabbi Isaiah Di Trani the Elder discusses whether a blessing is required for the reading of the Scroll of Antiochus.

Although the Scroll of Antiochus agrees in most respects with the story that is told in the Books of Maccabees or in the works of Josephus Flavius, it also contains some interesting differences. For one thing, it includes the talmudic tale about the jug of oil that burned miraculously for eight days (*Shabbat* 21b), a legend that is not found outside of the Babylonian Talmud. The scroll speaks of Judah Maccabee falling in battle during the lifetime of his father Mattathias, whereas all the other records claim that Mattathias died before the outbreak of the revolt.

No doubt the addition of a mandatory recitation of a Hanukkah Megillah into our own holiday prayers would go a long way towards increasing our knowledge of the Maccabean revolt and its significance. Nevertheless, I fear that our congregations will not take kindly to any further lengthening of a synagogue service that is already distinguished by special additions like the Hallel and the *Al Ha-Nissim*.

Perhaps the public reading of the Scroll would appear more attractive if congregants were encouraged to respond with catcalls and noisemakers to every mention of the name "Antiochus," as is customary whenever the villain Haman's name is mentioned during the reading of the Scroll of Esther on Purim.

Suggestions for Further Reading

Atlas, S., and M. Perlmann. "Saadya on the Scroll of the Hasmoneans." *Proceedings of the American Academy for Jewish Research* 14 (1944): 1–23.

Fried, Nathan. "Nosah 'Ivri Hadash Shel Megilat Antiokhos." *Sinai* 64 (1969): 97–140.

Golinkin, David. "Hanukkah Exotica: On the Origin and Development of Some Hanukkah Customs." *Conservative Judaism* 53, no. 2 (2001): 41–50.

Kaddari, M. Z. "Megillat Antiokhos Ha-Aramit." *Bar-Ilan Annual* 2 (1964): 211–13.

Rosenthal, F. "Saadyah's Introduction to the Scroll of the Hasmoneans." *Jewish Quarterly Review* 36 (1945–46): 297–302.

Assideans for Everyone*

It was the Hasmonean family under the leadership Judah Maccabee, who succeeded in removing the yoke of Greek oppression and purifying the defiled Temple in Jerusalem.

However, they were not the first group to take up arms against Antiochus and the Hellenizers in defence of Jewish tradition.

According to the Books of Maccabees (1 Maccabees 2:42), there had been a prior attempt at Jewish resistance, spearheaded by a group called the "Assideans." There is no doubt that this term, which is preserved only in Greek transliteration, reflects the original Hebrew word *Hasidim*, "pious ones." Although the Hasidim fought fiercely for their cause, and were successful in their initial campaigns, the Greeks soon discovered their Achilles heel: As long as the devout freedom fighters refused to wage war on the Sabbath, they were setting themselves up as easy targets, and their ranks were soon decimated by a series of Saturday massacres (2:32–38).

* *The Jewish Free Press*, Calgary, December 7, 2001, pp. 22–24.

The turning point in the Hanukkah story occurred when Mattathias the Hasmonean ruled that it was permissible to wage defensive warfare on Shabbat (2:39–41). Once Mattathias and his sons had taken charge of the military campaign, the remaining loyalist forces joined the Hasmonean resistance, and little was heard afterwards from the Assideans as a separate group.

It is widely believed that the biblical Book of Daniel was composed by these Assideans. Although the book is ostensibly relating stories that occurred centuries earlier, in the Babylonian courts of Nebuchadnezzar and Belshazzar, it reflects the historical situation and Jewish religious values at the time of the Hellenistic persecutions.

Employing a bizarre symbolic language of dreams and mythic beasts, Daniel tells of a supremely evil empire that will arise and oppress God's faithful. So invincible will this empire be that it can be brought low only through direct intervention by the Almighty himself, and not by any human agency. When God finally steps in to take an active part in the course of history, he will bring to a climax the succession of wicked kingdoms, and thereby initiate a radical new age in which humans will finally live in accordance with God's will.

The themes described here express eloquently what must have been the dominant mood among the Jewish faithful during the early stages of the Hanukkah story. The Hellenizing traitors seemed invincible, and there was no suggestion that their successes would ever cease; while the laws of the Torah were being trampled with impunity.

The author of Daniel provided assurances to his beleaguered readers that God would not allow this situation to continue perpetually. The tables would soon be turned, and those who maintained their faith under adversity would eventually be vindicated when God exacted vengeance on the sinners.

The historical records tell us almost nothing about the Assideans as a religious movement, other than the basic facts of their struggle against Hellenists and the unfortunate consequences of their strict Sabbath observance. They seem to have maintained some measure of distinct identity even after joining up with the Maccabean forces. At a later stage in the events, they fell victim to another unfortunate policy choice when (unlike Judah Maccabee) they consented to acknowledge the authority of the Hellenizing Jewish High Priest Alcimus. The latter returned the favour by slaughtering sixty of the Hasidim (1 Maccabees 7:13–16).

As often occurs in scholarship, the scarcity of solid facts serves as an open invitation to later generations to flesh out the details with hefty doses of imagination and ideological bias. In surveying the last two centuries of historiographical writing, one is overwhelmed by the confidence with which writers were able to describe the beliefs and values of the enigmatic movement of the Pious.

For several traditional Jewish historians, it was obvious that the ancient Hasidim were the forerunners of the type of Judaism that would later be known as Rabbinic. Some writers went so far as to identify by name the movement's founder: Simeon the Just, one of the earliest known names in the chain of transmitters of the oral Torah. Proponents of this view drew support from the fact that the Talmud makes occasional references to a group that it calls "Hasidim of early times." Another obscure figure from the Mishnah, Yosé ben Jo'ezer of Seredah, is designated a *Hasid*, and a tradition recorded in the Midrash includes him among the victims of Alcimus' treachery (*Genesis Rabbah* 65:22).

A markedly different picture emerges from the writings of some secular Jewish scholars. One of the most distinguished historians of the Hellenistic era asserted with unwavering certainty that the Assideans/Hasideans should be seen not merely as defenders of ancestral religious traditions, but as the champion of socio-economic class interests.

According to this view, the revolt against the Greeks was nothing less than a Marxist class struggle, with the pious Hasideans representing the interests of the urban populace of Jerusalem, including craftsmen, workers, and petty traders. As one historian put it: "The law of Moses ... became the war-cry of the masses, just as Greek culture was the watchword of the aristocracy. When the urban *plebs* took up arms to oppose the Hellenizing government with force, it was natural that the Hasidim ... should be the popular directors and leaders of the insurrection."

What a convenient coincidence that those ancient pietists, as depicted by these historians, were motivated by the same socialist ideology that guided the Labour-Zionist pioneers of the twentieth century!

In much recent scholarship, the view has taken hold that the Hasideans were an ascetic, non-violent group who later evolved into the Essene movement that withdrew from Jerusalem to pursue a life of spiritual purity in the Judean desert. This reconstruction has been copied so often from writer to writer that it seems to have achieved the status of confirmed fact.

What is exasperating about this claim is not simply that it lacks documentary corroboration. In actuality, it utterly contradicts the few facts that are known about the Hasideans. After all, they were mentioned chiefly as a military group who waged a war (albeit an unsuccessful one) against the Hellenizing forces! The Book of Maccabees speaks of them as "mighty men in Israel," and it requires some chutzpah to interpret this expression as an allusion to spiritual prowess. Only an obstinate disregard for the sources would allow them to be portrayed as ascetic pacifists.

It would appear that this audacious twist of scholarly fantasy is symptomatic of a more general pattern among historical writers. It reflects the desperate quest of Christians to uncover roots of their faith in earlier forms of Judaism. After working so hard to dissociate themselves from the "arid legalism" of Pharisaic and rabbinic religion, they turned their attention to less prominent sects of the Second Jewish Commonwealth.

On the whole, this scholarly enterprise led to far-reaching misrepresentations of the Essenes, the Hasidim, the Pharisees, and for that matter, the early Christians.

When all is said and done, what is most extraordinary about this episode is the inexplicable attraction that the ancient Hasideans have continued to exert upon later generations. In their own time, it is true, they were pushed to the sidelines of history, defeated by their enemies and superseded by the Hasmoneans.

Nevertheless, recent generations have been competing vigorously to claim them as their spiritual ancestors.

Suggestions for Further Reading

Finkelstein, Louis. *The Pharisees, the Sociological Background of their Faith.* 3rd ed., *Morris Loeb series.* Philadelphia: Jewish Publication Society of America, 1962.

Sandmel, Samuel. *Judaism and Christian Beginnings.* New York: Oxford University Press, 1978.

Tcherikover, Victor. *Hellenistic Civilization and the Jews.* 1st ed. Philadelphia: Jewish Publication Society of America, 1959.

Vermès, Géza. *Discovery in the Judean Desert,* New York: Desclee, 1956.

———. *The Complete Dead Sea Scrolls in English,* London: Penguin, 1995.

The Fifteenth of Sh'vat

This midwinter date was originally set down in the Talmud as a criterion for determining the age of trees, with reference to various agricultural regulations from the Bible. In the allegorical interpretations of the sixteenth-century Kabbalists, this "birthday of the trees" acquired the characteristics of a holiday in its own right. With the rise of Zionism, "Tu Bi-Sh'vat" has taken on additional trappings of a festival that celebrates nature and the connection of the Jewish people to their ancestral soil.

Apples and Apocalypse*

The talmudic sages (*Rosh Hashanah* 1:1) designated a "new year for the trees" in order to identify the agricultural year to which a fruit crop belongs, for purposes of tithing regulations. There is no evidence from ancient Rabbinic literature that the Fifteenth of Sh'vat was ever celebrated as a holiday with distinctive observances or customs.

Shortly after the close of the talmudic era we begin to discern a tendency for the Fifteenth of Sh'vat to assimilate certain attributes of the *real* New Year, Rosh Hashanah

Liturgical poems. from the Land of Israel, entreating the Almighty to bestow his blessings upon the fruits of the trees, were composed in order to embellish the prayers on the Fifteenth of Sh'vat. This evidence suggests that the Jews of the Holy Land, who lived off the soil and for whom the flourishing of the crops was a crucial matter of daily sustenance, were the first to observe the New Year of the Trees as a veritable holiday.

* *The Jewish Free Press*, Calgary, January 20, 2000, pp. 8–9.

Perhaps we are justified in tracing a thread of continuity between the older Israeli practice and the customs of the medieval Ashkenazic communities. The pioneering leader of German Jewry, the tenth-century Rabbi Gershom, known as the "Light of the Exile," dealt in one of his responsa with the advisability of ordaining a series of communal fast days that would overlap the Fifteenth of Sh'vat. Rabbi Gershom declares that in such a case it would be preferable to postpone the fast, rather than violate the festive character of the trees' New Year which, after all, is equated in talmudic literature with Rosh Hashanah.

Later chroniclers of Ashkenazic customs, including Rabbi Jacob Moelin (the Maharil) noted as well that penitential prayers are omitted on the Fifteenth of Sh'vat, in recognition of the date's festive status.

By the sixteenth century we hear accounts that Ashkenazic Jews were commemorating the trees' New Year with a special ritual: the eating of fruits. This practice was recorded in the Yiddish *Book of Customs* (*Minhagim Bukh*) that was printed in 1590 in Venice and subsequently reissued in several European centres. A seventeenth-century authority even recorded that in Worms, Germany, it was customary to cancel school on this date, and that the teachers were expected to treat their charges to liquor and cakes.

Until this time, there is virtually no mention of these practices among Sepharadic Jews. Neither Maimonides' comprehensive twelfth-century code of Jewish law nor the Kabbalistic traditions from the circle of Rabbi Isaac

Luria in sixteenth-century Safed contain any references to the observance of the Fifteenth of Sh'vat as a holiday.

For Jews in the Sepharadic diaspora, a decisive turning point occurred at the close of the seventeenth century with the publication of a work of Kabbalistic pietism that bore the name *Hemdat Yamim* ["the Beloved of Days"]. Deeply imbued with the esoteric teachings of Luria's school, the author of *Hemdat Yamim* drew upon a rich library of earlier works in order to attach Kabbalistic symbolism to all the days of the Jewish sacred calendar.

The *Hemdat Yamim* was the first book to set forth an elaborate Passover-like *seder* for the Fifteenth of Sh'vat, built around the ceremonial tasting of thirty different fruits from the Land of Israel. The consumption of each fruit was accompanied by the recitation of appropriate texts from the Bible, Talmud, and Zohar.

Underlying all these texts was an intense yearning for messianic redemption: When the exiled children of Israel return to their native soil, the blossoming of the fruit from the earth serves as a model for the hoped-for resurgence of the Jewish nation.

Hemdat Yamim was exceptionally influential, and it quickly gained acceptance among Jewish communities throughout North Africa, Europe, Turkey, the Balkans, and central Asia. The seder for the Fifteenth of Sh'vat was later published separately under the title *P'ri Etz Hadar* ["the fruit of a goodly tree"] and became the basis for the celebration of the day in all Sepharadic and oriental Jewish congregations.

It is not surprising that the intense messianic craving that was embodied in the *Hemdat Yamim* ceremony struck a responsive chord in the hearts of Jews. However, there is still something extraordinary in the fact that this work should have been allowed to exert such a powerful influence on mainstream Jewish religious practice.

For, though the name of *Hemdat Yamim's* author has not yet been determined with certainty, there is one fact about him that remains uncontestable: He was a fervent follower of the seventeenth-century messianic pretender Shabbetai Zvi. The author's Sabbatian leanings were made amply clear in his poetic tributes to the movement's leader and to its prophet, Nathan of Gaza. These allusions were pointed out at the time by Rabbi Jacob Emden of Altona and other opponents of the Sabbatian heresy. In fact, many Sepharadic writers came to presume that Nathan was the author. Several writers even came to refer to Nathan respectfully as "Rabbi *Hemdat Yamim*."

The upshot of all this is that thousands of Jews who participate each year in their traditional Tu Bish'vat Seder, and find in it a vivid expression of their mystical longing for redemption, are in reality reciting words that were intended to proclaim the messiahship of Shabbetai Zvi.

It would appear that the borderline between orthodoxy and heresy is not always as clearly delineated as we might have wished. The diverse expressions of Jewish tradition have branched off in many surprising twists and turns – but they rarely fail to bear delicious and fascinating fruit.

SUGGESTIONS FOR FURTHER READING

Scholem, Gershom. "Veha-Ta'alumah Be'einah 'Omedet," *Behinot* 8 (1955): 79–95.

———. *Researches in Sabbateanism*, edited by A. Shapira, *Kitvei Gersom Scholem*, Tel-Aviv: Am Oved, 1991.

Tishby, I. *Netivei Emunah U-Minut, Sifiriyyat Makor*, Ramat-Gan: Agudat Ha-Soferim Be-Yisra'el and Masada, 1964.

Yaari, A. "Toledot Rosh Ha-shanah La-ilan," *Mahanayim* 42 (19600: 15–24.

It Grows on Trees*

I still retain some vivid childhood memories of the weeks preceding Tu Bish'vat, the Jewish New Year of the Trees. During this season, our normal obsession with collecting hockey cards would give way temporarily to a vigorous rivalry over which class in our school could purchase the greatest number of paper leaves.

Many of you will recall those little green adhesive leaves that were sold by the Jewish National Fund, designed to be stuck onto a picture of a many-branched tree. If the fierce competition between the classes in our school was at all typical, then the buy-a-leaf campaign must have been one very lucrative fundraising idea. It has inspired several more elaborate "tree of life" campaigns, variations of which have been implemented in our local institutions.

To tell the truth, the idea of selling artificial leaves did not originate with modern Zionism. The Mishnah (*Middot* 3:8) describes a golden grapevine that stood at the entrance to the sanctuary of the Jerusalem Temple.

* *The Jewish Free Press*, Calgary, February 8, 2001, pp. 10–11.

Prospective donors were encouraged to purchase leaves, grapes, or entire grape-clusters, which they could ceremoniously hang on the vine.

Maimonides emphasizes that the choice of a grapevine for this purpose had symbolic significance, since this was a favourite biblical metaphor for the people of Israel.

The Mishnah reports that the vine became so laden with gifts that it required three hundred priests to budge it. The Talmud, however, concedes that this number must be an exaggeration (*Hullin* 90b).

The Mishnah does not tell us whether the gold was put to any use, other than as a visual testimony to the people's devotion to God and the glory of the Temple. Most commentators, however, understood that it was accessed from time to time in order to defray expenses related to the upkeep of the Temple, to provide gold plating for the altar, or to support needy priests.

All these goals were clearly more noble than the uses to which golden fruits were being put in Greek mythology. One is reminded of the infamous apple that was given by Zeus to Paris of Troy. The young prince used it to reward Aphrodite for granting him the favours of fair Helen, setting in motion an unfortunate chain of events that would ultimately bring on the Trojan War.

The Mishnah quoted above was describing the situation that prevailed in the Second Temple. However, according to ancient Jewish legend, the idea of placing a golden plant in the sanctuary had already been implemented by King Solomon in the First Temple.

The main source for this tradition is a passage in 2 Chronicles 3:6 that enumerates the spectacular ornamentation in Solomon's edifice and adds the obscure remark that "the gold was gold of *parvaim*." The unique and mysterious Hebrew word *parvaim* was understood in various ways. Most commentators saw it as denoting a place name or a colour. However, a popular interpretation in the Midrash derived it from the Hebrew root meaning "fruitfulness," leading the rabbinic preachers to conclude that the golden ornaments of Solomon's Temple were actually alive and capable of bearing fruit. Rabbi Aha bar Isaac reported that "when Solomon constructed the Holy Temple, he fashioned inside it all sorts of trees. Whenever the trees outside would bear fruit, the ones inside also bore their fruit." When the fruits ripened and dropped from the boughs, they would be used for the livelihood of the priests [Jerusalem Talmud *Yoma* 4:4 (41d)].

One astute exegete explained that the gold fruits could not be plucked directly from the branches because no one knows how to tell when metal fruit is ripe enough to be picked. It was for this reason that they had to wait until they dropped off by themselves!

Some traditional commentators were uncertain whether the fruits produced by these trees were made of metal, or were of the normal edible variety.

The first-century Jewish historian Josephus Flavius may have been familiar with such fantastic traditions extolling the wondrous properties of King Solomon's golden plants. However, he took care to describe the phenomenon in strictly naturalistic terms, noting that their leaves were fashioned so finely and subtly that they gave the *illusion* of being in motion.

The miraculous animated gold was perceived by the sages of the Talmud as a reflection of Israel's proudest days of spiritual and national grandeur. Accordingly, the Midrash relates that their supernatural qualities ceased to operate when the Jews fell from glory or divine favour, either because of their lapse into idolatry in the days of King Manasseh, or with the intrusion of the Babylonian conquerors into the sacred precincts (*Numbers Rabbah* 12:4).

By the same token, however, the rabbis looked forward eagerly to the future days of messianic redemption, when the living golden fruit trees will once again be restored to the rebuilt Temple in Jerusalem.

And when that time comes, you may be certain that you will be receiving a call from the fundraisers asking you to pledge a leaf or a grape-cluster.

Renewable Resource*

Even in a land like Canada that is blessed with abundant, and apparently limitless, forests, we have come to appreciate what a precious commodity a tree can be. The Torah commanded that even in time of war, it is forbidden to destroy a fruit tree in order to build bulwarks against a besieged city.

The rabbis of the Talmud projected some of their own concerns for forestation back to the heroes of the Bible.

For example, in setting out the construction procedures for the Tabernacle, the Torah stipulates that much of the structure had to be fashioned from wooden boards (Exodus 25, etc.). The midrashic sages considered it quite surprising that so much lumber should have been available in the wastes of Sinai. They therefore inferred that the wood supply had been prepared far in advance, even before the Israelites were enslaved in Egypt.

The credit for such foresight was ascribed to the patriarch Jacob. When Jacob embarked on his journey to

* *The Jewish Free Press*, Calgary, January 24, 2002, p. 10.

join Joseph in Egypt, his prophetic vision and ancestral faith made him confident that his children would one day be redeemed from their exile and that they would be commanded to build a sanctuary in which to worship the Almighty.

Knowing how scarce timber is in the desert, Jacob took care to have his sons plant trees right away, so that they would be available centuries later when the need arose (*Genesis Rabbah* 94:4).

The rabbis found confirmation for this story in the wording of Exodus 25:15, where God commands, "you shall make the boards for the tabernacle of acacia wood *standing*." The apparently redundant word "standing" was understood as an allusion to the fact that the trees from which the boards were cut had been standing there previously.

Some midrashic traditions extolled the miraculous nature of these trees. For example, they applied to them the words of the Psalmist "then shall all the trees of the wood rejoice," implying that they burst into song when they were built into the tabernacle (*Tanhuma* ed. Buber, *Terumah* 9).

It should be noted that not all the rabbis took such an ecologically sensitive view of the origins of the tabernacle trees. An alternative midrashic tradition links the story to a different episode in Jacob's life, an unexpected detour that the patriarch made on his route to join Joseph in Egypt.

According to the Torah, Jacob first stopped off in Beersheba to offer sacrifices and to commune with his

Creator (Genesis 46:1). Rav Nahman claimed that Jacob also took advantage of the opportunity to cut down the tamarisk trees that Grandpa Abraham had planted there years before. It was these trees that Jacob set aside to be used for the Tabernacle (*Genesis Rabbah* 94:4).

At any rate, these traditions make the point that if trees are to be perceived as a renewable resource, we must view the matter over a broad time span, since the growth of a tree is likely to last several lifetimes. Unfortunately, not all people are capable of seeing beyond the immediate present.

An object lesson in the virtues of investing in future generations may be found in the story of the miracle-worker Honi ha-Me'aggel (*Hagigah* 23a).

Honi was once walking along the road when he encountered a man who was planting a carob tree. This struck Honi as an absurdly futile act. It takes a carob seventy years to mature, and the planter would not live to enjoy the fruits of his labour.

Upon hearing Honi's low opinion of his efforts, the man replied simply, "I found a world containing a carob tree. Just as my ancestors planted trees for my benefit, so shall I plant trees for the benefit of my descendants."

The tale goes on to describe how Honi sat down to eat his lunch, lay down to nap, and dozed off ... for seventy years.

When he finally awoke, he saw before him a man gathering fruit from a full-grown carob tree. Eventually, it was established that Honi was conversing with the grandson of the person who had originally planted the tree.

Though Honi's experience had evidently instilled in him an appreciation of how important it is to provide for the needs of future generations, his own end was a tragic one.

The brave new world in which he now found himself had no place for what it saw as a delusional old man who claimed to be the legendary Honi Ha-Me'aggel. Thrown into depression, he prayed for a quick death, and his wish was mercifully granted.

The sad case of Honi Ha-Me'aggel contains a large dose of poetic justice. Because his horizons were too limited to recognize his responsibilities to posterity, he was doomed to live in a bleak and inhospitable future.

Honi's tragic flaw was symbolized by his failure to appreciate the importance of planting a simple carob tree.

Purim

Purim [literally: the Feast of Lots] commemorates the events related in the biblical Book of Esther, where the Jews of the Persian empire were rescued from potential genocide at the hands of the evil Haman. The festival is celebrated by the reading of the scroll (*Megillah*) of Esther, feasting and gift-giving.

Passing through Shushan*

It is undoubtedly one of the most dramatic and tension-filled moments in the Book of Esther.

While the lives of Persia's Jews hang in the balance, Mordecai has persuaded Esther to risk her life by approaching the king, uninvited, to plead her people's cause. Esther has in turn beseeched her fellow Jews to fast and pray for three days for the successful outcome of her mission.

At this point, the story introduces an apparently superfluous detail into the sequence of events: "So Mordecai passed on, and did according to all that Esther had commanded him" (Esther 4:17).

What is the meaning of "passed on" here, and of what relevance is this item of information to the unfolding of the story?

Not surprisingly, the rabbis of the Talmud attempted to provide various explanations and translations for the obscure expression. Some read it in the sense of "transgressed," as an indication that Mordecai fasted on

* *The Jewish Free Press*, Calgary, March 12, 1998, pp. 6–7.

that day even though it was Passover according to their calculations, though such an activity would have been forbidden on a festival for anything less than a grave national emergency (*Megillah* 15a).

Among the suggestions mentioned in the Talmud is one by the third-century Babylonian sage Samuel: "He crossed over a stream of water."

Now this comment hardly helps to clarify the issue. Quite the contrary, Samuel has apparently introduced yet another irrelevant detail into the narrative. Rashi explains Samuel's statement as implying that Mordecai was on his way to assemble the Jews to pray for Esther. Though this interpretation may fit the context, it does not provide a satisfactory reason for mentioning the crossing of the stream.

Some of the most intriguing solutions to this puzzle do not come from the pens of scholars or exegetes, but from the chronicles of medieval Jewish travellers. Probably the most celebrated of that breed was the twelfth-century Spanish globetrotter Rabbi Benjamin of Tudela, whose detailed chronicle of his voyages among the Jewish communities of his day is one of our crucial sources of historical and demographic information about that era.

In his account of his visit to Shushan, the scene of the events related in Esther, Rabbi Benjamin remarks that "the River Tigris divides the city, and the bridge connects the two parts. On one side, where the Jews dwell, is the sepulchre of Daniel." (Daniel was of course an esteemed favourite son of the Persian Jews.)

From this account, we learn that the river separated Shushan's Jewish quarter, with its reported seven thousand inhabitants, from the royal palace, at least in Benjamin's days. A similar description is given by another celebrated medieval Jewish tourist, Petahiah of Regensburg, who visited Shushan at around the same time.

The fact that the palace, or Acropolis, of Shushan was separated from the city by a river is in fact known from ancient sources, including the geographer Strabo.

All this would indeed furnish corroboration for Rashi's version of the story, of how Mordecai had to traverse water in order to rally the Jewish community to its fasts and supplications.

This reconstruction of the local geography receives additional support from the commentary of Rabbi Abraham Ibn Ezra. Ibn Ezra's focus was not Mordecai's "passing on," but rather an apparent confusion in the terminology employed by the narrator in referring at times to "Shushan," and at times to "the palace of Shushan." This leads him to conclude that there were in reality two separate locations: the walled sector that contained the royal palace and the unwalled city that housed, among other things, the city's Jewish quarter.

As usual, Ibn Ezra's interpretation is based on thorough textual and linguistic analysis of the biblical evidence, though he does not tie it in with our problem about Mordecai's "passing on." However, it is also conceivable that his depiction of the ancient Persian capital reflected his experiences in Muslim Spain, where the caliphs were accustomed to constructing their magnificent palaces at a distance from the cities.

For all the attractiveness of the theory about Mordecai crossing a river to reach the Jewish neighbourhood, it still involves several difficulties.

For one thing, it supposes that the layout of the city's neighbourhoods remained substantially intact from the fifth century B.C.E. until the twelfth century C.E. While this is not entirely inconceivable in the slow-moving societies of pre-modern times, in this particular instance we have good reason to question the premise. References to a Jewish community in Shushan are entirely absent from talmudic sources, and a Persian document tells of the city's being completely rebuilt in the early fourth century C.E. by King Yezdegerd I – albeit at the request of his appropriately named Jewish queen, Shoshan-dukht, daughter of the reigning Exilarch.

Furthermore, we must recall that the entire interpretation hinges on Samuel's comment about Mordecai crossing a "stream" of water. Now, the Aramaic word that is used by Samuel to denote the body of water (*'urkama*) is one that appears in several passages in the Babylonian Talmud. If one compares how the word is used elsewhere, we find that the *'urkama* seems to refer to a mere puddle, or the temporary overflow from a river, rather than to the full-scale river that would be required by the aforementioned explanations.

When all is said and done, we still do not have a convincing solution to our original puzzle about Mordecai's movements in ancient Shushan. However, as is often the case, the search itself has been an educational experience all its own, allowing us to make the acquaintance of a diverse company of Jewish commentators, travellers, and even some royalty for good measure.

Exactly the sort of scholarly fare that is ideal for Purim.

Suggestions for Further Reading

Adler, Marcus Nathan, ed. *The Itinerary of Benjamin of Tudela: Critical Text, Translation and Commentary,* New York: Feldheim, 1907.

Eshel, Ben-Zion. *Jewish Settlements in Babylonia During Talmudic Times,* Jerusalem: The Magnes Press, 1979 [Hebrew].

Gafni, Isaiah M. *The Jews in Babylonia in the Talmudic Era: A Social and Cultural History,* edited by A. Grossman et al. Monographs in Jewish History. Jerusalem: Zalman Shazar Center, 1990 [Hebrew].

Hakham, Amos. "Esther," in *Hamesh Megillot,* Jerusalem: Mossad Harav Kook, 1973 [Hebrew].

Krauss, S. *Qadmoniyyot ha-Talmud.* Berlin, Vienna, Tel-Aviv, 1924–45.

Moore, C. A., ed. *Studies in the Book of Esther,* edited by H. M. Orlinsky. *The Library of Biblical Studies.* New York: Ktav, 1982.

———. ed. *Esther,* edited by W. F. Albright and D. N. Freedman. *The Anchor Bible.* Garden City: Doubleday, 1971.

Paton, Lewis Bayles. A Critical and Exegetical Commentary on the Book of Esther, International Critical Commentary. Edinburgh: T. & T. Clark, 1951.

Segal, Eliezer. *The Babylonian Esther Midrash: A Critical Commentary,* 3 vols., Brown Judaic Studies. Atlanta: Scholars Press, 1994.

Walfish, Barry. *Esther in Medieval Garb: Jewish Interpretation of the Book of Esther in the Middle Ages, SUNY Series in Judaica.* Albany, NY: State University of New York Press, 1993.

Troubles at Court*

The story might well have been lifted from the pages of *Ivanhoe*, if not from the Book of Esther itself.

Somewhere in France during the eleventh century, a Jewish woman was invited to go riding in the entourage of the local aristocracy. Presumably, such invitations were very rare, and it would have been a pity to forego such a festive occasion. Perhaps a refusal would even have been perceived as a rude insult to her blue-blooded hosts.

The problem was that the outing was scheduled for the eleventh of Adar. While this is not, strictly speaking, a Jewish holiday, such were the vicissitudes of the calendar that year that the eleventh of Adar was observed as the Fast of Esther.

Normally the fast is kept on the thirteenth of the month, the day immediately preceding Purim. That year, however, Purim fell on Sunday, and since it was not permitted to fast on the Sabbath, the fast had to be moved to a different day. Friday (the twelfth) was considered

* *The Jewish Free Press*, Calgary, February 25, 1999, pp. 12, 14.

inconvenient because it would interfere with Shabbat preparations. Therefore, the tradition had been established, in such infrequent circumstances, of observing the Fast of Esther on the Thursday preceding Purim, the eleventh of Adar.

So what should she do about the invitation to the riding party, whose physical exertions would certainly require some prior nourishment?

The case was brought before Rabbi Solomon ben Isaac, renowned as "Rashi," the leading halakhic authority of the day. On the surface, the religious obstacle did not appear overwhelming. It was not, after all, the real day of the fast, only a substitute. And the lady was not planning to avoid fasting altogether; she was merely asking whether she could postpone it to the next day.

Rashi's answer, however, was a flat refusal. The day, even in its transplanted date, was to be treated as a full-fledged statutory fast that could not be trifled with.

In issuing his ruling, the distinguished rabbi himself called attention to the questionable status of the Fast of Esther. It is mentioned neither in the Bible nor in the classical works of the Jewish oral tradition. It is a custom whose only known roots are in popular practice. However, for Rashi, as for most French and German halakhic authorities, popular customs were an incontestable foundation of Judaism.

We said that the fast has no source in the Bible. But does not the Book of Esther relate how the Jews of the Persian Empire fasted before the heroine approached Ahasuerus unannounced? Rashi argued that that fast had nothing to do with the one that we currently observe on the day before Purim. The biblical fast lasted three days, and took place in the month of Nissan, during Passover.

Rashi was aware that some commentators had tried to anchor the custom in the words of Esther 9:13, where Esther issued a decree concerning "the matters of the fastings and their cry." He refuted that proof-text. The verse plainly means that the annual holiday of Purim commemorates the tribulations and fastings of the ancient Persian Jews, not that Jews are to continue to fast every year. Otherwise, to be consistent, we would have to also "cry" on Purim, which is very obviously not done.

In light of the strong case that Rashi made for the non-biblical and non-talmudic status of the Fast of Esther, we might well ask why he was so intransigent about accommodating the lady's innocuous request.

His answer is a simple one: communal solidarity. It is unacceptable for individuals to maintain separate practices or to withdraw from the observances of the larger community. This is a fundamental axiom that governs much of classical Jewish law, especially in medieval Europe.

Rashi's criticisms were not limited to those who tried to omit or reschedule established practice. He also censured individuals who, out of excessive piety, insisted on observing a second fast day on Friday, in order to place it closer to Purim. This practice overstated the importance of the fast of Esther by elevating it to biblical status, and hence it was equally unacceptable.

It is clear that Rashi's argumentation falls within the standard parameters of halakhic discourse, as he bases his position on the relevant biblical and talmudic sources and legal principles, without relating to the specific personalities or historical circumstances involved in the case.

I am nevertheless tempted to speculate whether there might have been additional motives behind his attempt to prevent the lady from socializing with royalty. The story of Queen Esther notwithstanding, the blurring of accepted social and religious barriers could sometimes lead to unfortunate results.

A notorious instance occurred a century later, and not very far from Rashi's home. In the northern French community of Blois, a Jewish woman named Polcelina began to frequent the court of Count Theobald, and the relationship eventually developed romantic overtones. For as long as Polcelina was able to maintain her favoured status among the nobility, she became accustomed to lording it over her fellow Jews, who recognized their growing dependence on her political influence.

Eventually, however, the Count's affection for Polcelina began to diminish. She was taken prisoner at the behest of her political rivals and strictly forbidden to communicate with Count Theobald, for fear that her charms might again allow her to return to favour. Her fall from grace was initially welcomed by many members of the Jewish community, where her overbearing ways had succeeded in arousing considerable resentment.

Matters took a tragic turn in the spring of 1171. A Christian servant, aware of his master's current distaste for the former object of his affections, incensed perhaps by the vilification of the Jews that was a stock ingredient of the seasonal preaching, and provoked by the fact that that his horse had recently been frightened by a Jew, seized the opportunity to spread a baseless charge of ritual murder against the Jewish community of Blois.

The results were catastrophic. The irate count, deaf to the bribes that usually sufficed to avert such incidents, had more than thirty Jews burned on May 26, 1171. It was Rashi's own grandson, Rabbi Jacob Tam, who issued an enactment establishing the twentieth of Sivan as an annual fast day for the Jewish communities of France and the Rhineland. "It is fitting," he wrote, "that this date should be declared a day of fasting for all our people, more important even than the Fast of Gedaliah son of Ahikam, for it is a true day of atonement."

It is tempting to imagine that, in setting up halakhic obstructions to a Jewish woman's socializing with the French nobility, Rashi had anticipated a calamity just like the one that would be precipitated by Polcelina of Blois.

At any rate, the story does serve to teach us that it is not always a welcome development when a Jewish woman attracts the heart of a gentile ruler. Although it can be the occasion for the festive celebration of Purim, it might also lead to fasting and lamentation.

Suggestions for Further Reading

Chazan, R. "The Blois Incident of 1171: A Study in Jewish Intercommunal Organization," *Proceedings of the American Academy for Jewish Research* 36 (1968): 13–31.

———. *Medieval Jewry in Northern France: A Social and Political History,* Baltimore: Johns Hopkins University Press, 1973.

Elfenbein, I., ed. *Teshuvot RashI,* New York, 1943.

Spiegel, S. "Mippitgamei ha-'Aqedah: Serufei Blois ve-Hit-haddeshut 'Alilot ha-Dam." In *Mordecai M. Kaplan Jubilee Volume,* edited by M. Davis. New York: Jewish Theological Seminary of America, 1953.

The Purim-Shpiel and the Passion Play*

Since I have come to be perceived in certain circles as Calgary's resident authority on ancient Judaism, I was consulted by the staff of the Badlands Passion Play in Drumheller in their sincere resolve to imbue their production with historical accuracy. Needless to say, the situation elicits some very mixed and ironic emotions in me when I think of the sinister history of European passion plays. In the classic medieval versions of these productions, the Jews were invariably cast as demonic Christ-killers, and at the conclusions of the performance, the incensed audiences were ready to take out their wrath upon the local descendants of that depraved brood, resulting in violent attacks against innocent Jews.

Although we are much more familiar with the image of Jews as innocent victims of these riots, historians are now calling attention to a large body of circumstantial evidence which suggests that the reading of the Megillah on Purim played a reciprocal role of inciting Jews

* *The Jewish Free Press*, Calgary, March 16, 2000, pp. 12–13.

against Christians, even to the point of acts of violence or murder.

Evidence of this phenomenon can be traced as far back as the early Byzantine Empire, where the Emperor Theodosius, in his famous law code, felt it necessary to include a directive to the provincial governors instructing them to forbid the Jewish practice of burning an effigy of Haman on Purim, a figure that was perceived as a parody of the crucified Jesus.

Theodosius was of course the ruler of a Christian empire, and we might justifiably accuse him of slandering the Jews, or even of erroneously imagining an anti-Christian affront where none was intended. However, several considerations lend some credence to his suspicions.

Though we are accustomed to imagine Haman and his sons as hanging on a gallows from a noose, that manner of execution was evidently unknown in antiquity. The ancient Aramaic translations always render the word by the root *tzalab*, meaning "crucify." This, of course, was a common Roman form of capital punishment, and originally had no uniquely Christian associations. However, for later generations all references to crucifixion were naturally associated with that of Jesus.

Most Jews are aware that Haman was descended from the Amalek, that archetypal enemy of Israel. Our standard telling of the story tends to overlook the fact that the biblical Amalek was a descendent of Esau, whom midrashic tradition regarded as the prototype of the evil Roman Empire. With the Christianization of Rome, some Jews continued to apply the symbolism of Esau to the Christian church and to the Byzantine Empire that was so implacably hostile towards Judaism.

Shortly after the promulgation of the Theodosian Code in 438, an incident was reported in the Syrian town of Inmestar, when a mob of drunken Jews began blaspheming Christians and their messiah. They seized a Christian child, placed him on a cross, and began to make sport of him, eventually causing the boy's death. The circumstances make it likely that the unfortunate event occurred on Purim, and was inspired by the Jews' equation of Haman with Jesus or Christianity.

Again, we have good reason to suspect that the story is nothing more than an anti-Semitic fabrication.

Nevertheless, in medieval Byzantium, Jewish converts to Christianity were required to make a solemn declaration that they "anathematize those who celebrate the festival of Mordecai ... and those who nail Haman to a piece of wood, and joining it to the sign of the cross, burn them together while hurling various curses and anathemas against the Christians."

Here too, the accusations emanate from hostile sources, and our history is replete with such charges being levelled against us without any factual basis. It is entirely possible that malicious outside observers were ascribing imagined motives to the traditional Jewish condemnations of the biblical Haman.

Similar doubts arise when we read that in later times Christians continued to be offended by the fact that European Jewish communities would publicly disgrace their own sinners on Purim (a feature that was also central to the gentile carnivals of the time). It seems that Christians, used to viewing the present through the lens of their scriptures, automatically equated any Jewish act of public chastisement with the scourging of Jesus.

A particularly thorny problem is the following episode, which was related in widely differing versions by two independent Jewish chroniclers, as well as by a Christian writer:

In a French town named Bray [or: Brie]-sur-Seine, at the close of the twelfth century, a Christian attached to the royal court killed a Jew. The victim's family succeeded in bribing the local duchess to hand the perpetrator over to them to be hanged. According to the Christian reporter, the execution was preceded by a ceremonious procession through the town square during which the murderer had a crown of thorns placed on his head (in a transparent burlesque of Jesus' crucifixion). So incensed was King Philip Augustus upon hearing of this development that he ordered the martyrdom of the local Jewish community.

Here too the sources differ with reference to several of the salient details. Only one of the Hebrew reports states that the hanging took place on Purim, whereas the other one does not mention a hanging at all, but rather says that the resulting pogrom occurred on Purim (presumably in retaliation for the arrest of the Christian). The non-Jewish source dates the execution two weeks *after* Purim. Historians are in disagreement about how much credence to attach to each of the versions, though some have insisted that the story makes the most sense against the background of the chauvinism and general license that characterized the medieval Purim celebrations.

I am personally inclined to see this as another instance of Christians permanently typecasting the Jews as the bloodthirsty taunters of their messiah. However, in light of the repeated tendency of Jews to equate Haman or Amalek with their contemporary enemies, one can sympathize with those historians who attach greater weight to the reports.

In fact, this might be the real moral of the story: When religious or ideological communities begin to perceive each other as symbolic archetypes, rather than as living, breathing human beings, then it is only a matter of time until they start treating each other inhumanly. At that point, both the Passion Play and the Purim-shpiel are transformed into regrettable tragedies.

Suggestions for Further Reading

Chazan, Robert. "The Bray Incident of 1192: *Realpolitik* and Folk Slander." *Proceedings of the American Academy for the Advancement of Jewish Research* 37 (1969): 1–18.

Doniach, N. S. *Purim, or the Feast of Esther: An Historical Study.* Philadelphia: Jewish Publication Society of America, 1933.

Horowitz, Elliott. "'And It Was Reversed': Jews and Their Enemies in the Festivities of Purim," *Zion* 59 (2–3) (1994): 129–68.

Roth, Cecil. "The Feast of Purim and the Origins of the Blood Accusation." In *The Blood Libel Legend: A Casebook in Anti-Semitic Folklore,* edited by A. Dundes. Madison: University of Wisconsin Press, 1991.

Thornton, T. C. G. "The Crucifixion of Haman and the Scandal of the Cross," *Journal of Theological Studies* 37 (1986): 420–29.

The Wise King Ahasuerus*

In our democratic world, the role of the sovereign has become a questionable one, particularly in constitutional monarchies where their role is confined to the ceremonial and symbolic.

The story of Purim has provided Jewish scholars through the ages with occasions to contemplate the nature of government, and the place of the king within the mechanisms of power. Their interpretations of the biblical text often reveal a great deal about their own contemporary concerns.

I think that modern readers have tended to regard Ahasuerus as something of a comical buffoon. This is not only the result of the frivolity that has characterized our Purim celebrations, but it legitimately reflects the king's ever-changing positions in the Esther narrative. Initially, he is a benevolent leader entertaining the populace with banquets and festivities. Quickly he is persuaded by Haman to support a genocidal massacre. And then, just as instantly, Esther converts him into an ally of the Jews,

* *Ha-Atid: Magazine of the Melbourne Hebrew Congregation*, Melbourne Australia, 4:2 (14) 14–15, March–May 2000.

determined to execute vengeance on Haman and his collaborators.

It is difficult not to agree with the talmudic rabbis who termed Ahasuerus a *hafakhfakhan,* an unstable personality easily influenced by his counsellors and subject to constant changes of attitude (*Megillah* 15b).

A recurring argument in the Talmud concerns the evaluation of Ahasuerus' intelligence. Was he a shrewd statesman, or an incompetent boob? Certain episodes lend themselves to either interpretation.

Thus, the opening verses of Esther (1:3–5) recount two separate royal feasts. In the first, the king entertained the citizens of the provinces, and only afterwards did he convene celebrations for the residents of Shushan, the capital city. Some rabbis were convinced that it was a wise political move to curry the goodwill of the outsiders first, while others insisted that it was an act of folly to befriend the provincials, who might rebel at any moment, before he had properly secured his position at home (*Megillah* 12a).

Several talmudic sages were quick to adduce examples of Ahasuerus' stupidity and fickleness: in his abandonment of former allies, in his impulsive treatment of Vashti, and in several other displays of dubious judgment.

In light of this critical attitude among the ancient Jewish sages, it comes as something of a surprise to observe how determined many of the medieval commentators were to paint the Persian king in flattering colours.

This was particularly true among scholars who lived in Spain.

Even with regard to that most incriminating of passages, when Ahasuerus gives Haman a *carte blanche* to eradicate the Jews of the empire, several Spanish Jewish exegetes insisted that the king did not really intend that the Jews should come to physical harm.

Thus, Rabbi Abraham Ḥadidah argued that the king only planned to destroy the Jews' possessions, but not to kill the people. According to this interpretation, when Haman subsequently issued the order "to destroy, to kill, and to cause to perish, all Jews, both young and old" (Esther 3:13), he was exceeding the authority that had been granted to him by the king. For this reason, Ahasuerus could sincerely claim later on that he had been completely unaware of Haman's machination.

In a similar vein, Rabbi Isaac Arama wrote that Ahasuerus' scheme had been to expel the Jews from his domains, rather than to murder them. Clearly Rabbi Arama had in mind the recent experiences of several European Jewish communities, in England, France, and elsewhere, who had been forcibly evicted from their respective lands.

Another Spanish interpreter, Rabbi Abraham Saba, could not conceive of the possibility that an emperor of Ahasuerus' great stature would knowingly perpetrate a ruthless massacre. To do so would bring lasting shame upon his kingdom, and no self-respecting king would contemplate it. Rabbi Isaac Arama concurred, insisting that the very possibility of murdering an entire nation was so abhorrent to human nature that no monarch would have given such an order.

According to some other commentators, the king's sympathies for his Jewish subjects were assured by their indispensable contributions to the royal coffers. It would be an act of economic irresponsibility to eliminate such a lucrative source of tax revenues. Rabbi Solomon Astruc argued that in the closing verses of the Megillah, when "king Ahasuerus laid a tribute upon the land, and upon the isles of the sea," he was in fact following Mordecai's advice in levying a tax on the Jews, as a way of underscoring their fiscal benefits to the realm.

This irrational desire to defend Ahasuerus, to a degree that is unwarranted by the biblical account or its midrashic interpretations, seems to accurately reflect the attitudes of many Jews towards their own monarchs. Under the prevailing rules of medieval politics, the Jews were the "property" of the king, or of the royal treasury, and enjoyed the direct protection of the Crown. When anti-Jewish hostilities were incited by other segments of the society, whether from the nobility, the clergy, or the peasantry, it was the king who was responsible for guaranteeing the security of "his Jews." The monarchs usually lived up to their obligations, but not always.

At any rate, the ability of the Jews to maintain their fragile existence as a despised minority within a hostile environment depended on their ability to convince themselves of the faithfulness, not only of their current rulers, but of the institution of monarchy itself. If they could not depend on their kings, then who knew what might befall them?

In the end, as we all know, the latter-day Ahasuerus-es into whose hands they had entrusted their destinies betrayed them; and the glorious Jewish communities of the Iberian Peninsula were destroyed overnight, with the blessing of the monarchy, by means of expulsions, massacres, and forced conversions.

Of course, from our post-Holocaust perspective the patriotic self-delusion exhibited by the Spanish Jewish commentators appears pathetic, if not pathological. It reminds us of the naiveté of those German and Polish Jews who upheld their faith in the decency of European Enlightenment until the bitter end.

And yet, it is difficult to know if we would have acted differently under the circumstances. Only in recent years have the Jewish communities of the United States and Canada become aware how our governments, while maintaining public postures of liberality and benevolence, were in fact hard at work suppressing all reports of Nazi genocide, and ensuring that no Jewish refugees would find refuge on our hospitable shores. At the same time, Her Majesty's Government in the United Kingdom was making additional efforts to keep the Jews out of Palestine, for fear of alienating their Middle-Eastern allies.

Through all those years of betrayal, the Jews of these enlightened lands continued to maintain unwavering faith in the uprightness of their leaders. Any alternative was unimaginable.

I expect that future generations of Jews will continue to examine the story of Purim from the perspective of their own experiences. Even after the last despicable Haman has vanished from the earth, the events and personalities of the Book of Esther will inspire us to insightful discussions about the ideals of good government.

Suggestions for Further Reading

Walfish, Barry. *Esther in Medieval Garb: Jewish Interpretation of the Book of Esther in the Middle Ages. SUNY Series in Judaica.* Albany, NY: State University of New York Press, 1993.

Esther and the Essenes*

One of the many riddles that have been posed by the Dead Sea Scrolls is the apparent absence of any complete or partial copy of the Book of Esther. The thousands of fragments in that ancient library include the oldest known texts of the Hebrew Bible, some of them (like a scroll of Isaiah) in relatively complete form, but most of them in tiny shreds and crumbs.

Only Esther is missing.

As long as a large proportion of the scrolls remained unclassified and unpublished, it was possible to argue that the anomaly was only temporary, and that Esther fragments would eventually surface among newly identified texts. However, in recent years, as the pace of publication has accelerated, the situation has not changed, and we are no closer than ever to a solution.

Unable to discover actual texts of Esther, the experts scurried to find indirect hints that the book was known and studied by the Essenes, the sect who are widely believed to have written or preserved the Dead

* *The Jewish Free Press*, Calgary, March 8, 2001, pp. 12–13.

Sea Scrolls. For example, one scholar examined the work known as the "Genesis Apocryphon," an Aramaic expansion of the lives of the Hebrew Patriarchs, and noted some similarities between its account of Sarah's sojourn in Pharaoh's palace and the Scriptural story of Esther's exploits in the court of Ahasuerus. Unfortunately, the alleged similarities were quite tenuous, and were based on a speculative reconstruction of the original Hebrew from translations.

An apparent turning point in the discussion came in 1992 with the initial publication of a poorly preserved Aramaic text. The text's editor, J. T. Milik, was struck by remarkable similarities between certain expressions in this newly discovered work and the language and themes of Esther.

To cite some of the more salient parallels: The Qumran document relates events that took place in the Persian imperial court. King Darius is mentioned, evidently as the father of the currently reigning monarch. If the reference is to the first king to bear that name, then that would make him the father of Xerxes, who was the Ahasuerus of the Bible.

In Milik's text, as in Esther, is found an episode involving the reading before the king of a royal chronicle that speaks of the loyalty of one of the protagonists in his service for the king.

Individual phrases in the Qumran document also demonstrate resemblances to expressions that occur in the Book of Esther. "The fear of the house of the scribe fell upon him" sounds like Esther 8:17: "the fear of the

Jews fell upon them." More significantly, one of the characters identifies himself as "a man of Judah, one of the leaders of Benjam[in ...] an exile," a formula that distinctly evokes the Bible's description of Mordecai as "a man of Judah, ... a Benjaminite, who had been carried away from Jerusalem with the captivity."

Unfortunately, no actual names from the Esther story appear in the Qumran text, a fact that caused immense frustration to the editors. Prof. Milik, in his determination to establish a connection with Esther, was not above forcibly inserting appropriate names into his text. Thus, a single surviving *alef* in a torn passage provided him with sufficient grounds for completing the word as "Esther." In another place, a *yod* was read as the first letter of *Jair*, Mordecai's father. One of the antagonists in the Dead Sea fragment was apparently named "Hama," and Milik could not resist the temptation to equate him with the biblical Haman. However, since Hama was spelled with a Hebrew *het* and Haman with a *he*, it became necessary to hypothesize that our biblical text was based on a second-hand Greek translation! In a similar spirit, a word that should apparently be read as *saretah*, meaning a princess, was identified by Milik as Haman's wife Zeresh.

I believe that these examples should suffice to indicate the lengths to which people were ready to go in order to find Esther at Qumran.

Several other scholars, well aware of the critical divergences between Esther and Milik's Dead Sea document, were content to lump them together with works such as Daniel or the Joseph story in Genesis, as instances of a more general "Jewish courtier in a foreign court" genre. Some, however, went so far as to claim that the Qumran fragment preserves the original "proto-Esther" out of which our beloved biblical book evolved!

In reality, the Qumran text is most conspicuous for the large number of names that have no parallel in Esther at all. Most of these exotic names have an authentic Persian flavour to them, such as Patireza, Bagoshe, or Bagasraw.

More significantly, the main antagonist in the Qumran document is designated a "Cuthite," that is, a Samaritan. Samaritans are not mentioned at all in Esther, where the villain Haman is identified as an "Agagite" (from the royal dynasty of Amalek).

I think that it is precisely this last-mentioned detail that provides us with the key to understanding the Qumran text.

The Bible records an acrimonious dispute that arose when Jewish and Samaritan delegations pleaded their respective case before the Persian government. However, this dispute is described, not in Esther, but in the Book of Ezra.

The Jews who returned from Babylonia to Zion, in response to Cyrus' proclamation, set to work rebuilding the Jerusalem Temple, but under the reign of Xerxes they suffered a major setback. The hostile Samaritans issued a protest to the Persian governor, resulting in the suspension of construction for the duration of Xerxes' reign. The intrigues depicted in the Dead Sea document make much more sense when viewed against that background.

There is nevertheless an indirect connection to Esther. The two episodes occurred at the same time, and the same Xerxes-Ahasuerus was involved in both. This point was given special emphasis in the talmudic and midrashic traditions, where the postponement of the Temple's reconstruction occupied a central place in the rabbis' retelling of the Esther story. A popular legend identified "Shimshai the scribe," one of the leading instigators of the Samaritan opposition, as the son of the wicked Haman (*Megillah* 16a).

In spite of our skepticism regarding some of these scholarly arguments, there are enough Esther-like phrases scattered among the Dead Sea Scrolls to establish beyond reasonable doubt that the Essenes were familiar with its contents. If this is true, then it only serves to heighten the mystery of the book's absence from the Qumran library.

Upon further reflection, however, we can appreciate that the austere Essenes would have looked askance at many aspects of the Megillah. Taken at face value, Esther appears to be a disturbingly secular – or even profane – story, in which God's name is never invoked, and the salvation of the Jews is achieved through a combination of shrewd scheming, personal courage, and fortuitous coincidence. For the fatalistic folk at Qumran, who believed that human destiny is meticulously predetermined by the Almighty, this was not an acceptable message.

The folks at Qumran would also have been uneasy about the cosmopolitan ambience that pervades the Esther story. Not only do the Jews of Shushan mingle freely in the Persian court and partake in the (apparently non-kosher) feasting and drinking, but the heroine, with scarcely a thought about the halakhic implications, takes the unthinkable step of marrying the heathen monarch. This would have caused serious discomfort to the insular and xenophobic Essenes, whose universe was neatly divided between the Children of Light (that is, themselves) and the Children of Darkness (everybody else).

Furthermore, The central role assigned to Esther in the Megillah would have grated on Essene sensibilities. Josephus Flavius reports that women were excluded from their community on account of their low opinion of female moral standards.

Under the circumstances, it might not really be so difficult to account for the absence of Esther from the Qumran library.

It is perfectly consistent with their general attitude that Esther should be heard ... but not Essene.

Suggestions for Further Reading

Ben-Dov, Jonathan. "A Presumed Citation of Esther 3:7 in 4Qdb." *Dead Sea Discoveries* 6 (1999): 282–84.

Crawford, Sidnie White. "Has Esther Been Found at Qumran? *4QProto-Esther* and the Esther Corpus." *Revue de Qumran* 17 (1996): 307–25.

De Troyer, Kristin. "Once More, the So-Called Esther Fragments of Cave 4." *Revue de Qumran* 19, no. 3 (2000): 401–22.

Eisenman, Robert H., and Michael Owen Wise. *The Dead Sea Scrolls Uncovered*. Shaftesbury: Element, 1992.

Finkel, J. "The Author of the Genesis Apocryphon Knew the Book of Esther." In *Essays on the Dead Sea Scrolls in Memory of E. L. Sukenik*, edited by C. Rabin and Y. Yadin. Jerusalem: Hekhal Ha-Sefer, 1961 [Hebrew].

Milik, J. T. "Les Modèles Araméens du Livre d'Esther dans la Grotte 4 de Qumran," *Revue de Qumran* 15 (1992): 321–406.

Talmon, Shemaryahu. "Was the Book of Esther Known at Qumran?," *Dead Sea Discoveries* 2 (1995): 249–68.

Remembering Harbona – for Good or for Bad?*

At the conclusion of the Megillah reading, it is customary to read a Hebrew poem that celebrates the victory of the Jews over their adversaries. Afterwards, several benedictions and brickbats are musically distributed to the heroes and villains of the story: Blessings are heaped upon Mordecai and Esther, while Haman and his wife Zeresh are singled out for malediction.

And as an anticlimax, the song concludes: "And Harbona too should be remembered for good."

Now, Harbona was hardly the most memorable figure in the Megillah. Altogether, he makes two brief walk-on appearances. The first time (1:10), he is mentioned as one of the seven chamberlains who advised Ahasuerus to exhibit Vashti before the guests at the royal banquet. Later, after Esther has pointed the accusing finger at Haman, it is Harbona who volunteers the information about the incriminating gallows that the villain has erected in his house (7:9), laying the groundwork for Haman to be hoist with his own petard.

* *The Jewish Free Press*, Calgary, February 7, 2002, pp. 10–11.

Considering how minor a character he is, it is quite surprising that he is given star billing in the closing credits, right up there beside Esther and Mordecai.

What is even more surprising is that the Babylonian Talmud had some very derogatory things to say about Harbona's apparent support for the good guys (*Megillah* 16a). According to Rabbi Hama bar Hanina, Harbona was initially a wicked collaborator in Haman's conspiracy. and only switched sides at the very last minute, when it was already evident that their plot was doomed to failure. His decision to become Witness for the Prosecution was, according to Rabbi Hama, nothing more than the desperate act of an opportunist, and not an expression of sympathy for the persecuted Jews.

Some of the traditional commentators were troubled by Rabbi Hama's readiness to cast aspersions on Harbona's character, seeing that the Bible itself offers no indication that the chamberlain was motivated by anything other than virtue and honesty. They scoured the text of the Megillah for clues that might point to his nefarious intentions.

Rabbi Samuel Eidels (the Maharsha) found just such a clue in the way that Harbona is identified as a servant of the king when he makes his first appearance, but not later on in the story. Perhaps, suggests Rabbi Eidels, this indicates that Harbona had shifted his allegiance in the interval from the king to Haman.

In a similar vain, Rabbi Josiah Pinto pointed out that the biblical text is very careful to state that Harbona made his accusation of Haman "before the king" – as if to imply that prior to that point his words had not been addressed to the king, but to Haman.

Rabbi Solomon Alkabetz draws our attention to a tiny inconsistency in the way Harbona's name is spelled in the two places where it is mentioned. The first time, it ends with an *alef* and the second time with a *he*. This, he concludes, must have been the author's subtle way of teaching us that Harbona had undergone a change of heart during the course of the narrative.

These negative evaluations of Harbona's character and motives do not help to explain why our traditional liturgy is so willing to bestow blessings upon him.

It would appear that not all the ancient Jewish sages were in agreement with Rabbi Hama bar Hanina's disparaging view of Harbona. Our current practice follows the ruling of a certain Rabbi Pinhas in the Jerusalem Talmud [*Megillah* 3:7 (74b)], who stated "one must say: Harbona of blessed memory."

Rabbi Pinhas's statement appears in several midrashic and halakhic works that were composed in the Land of Israel (e.g., *Genesis Rabbah* 49:1), and it seems to reflect the prevailing view there, As was the case with many ancient Israeli customs, this one too became the normative practice among the Jews of medieval France and Germany.

According to one midrashic tradition (*Esther Rabbah* 10:9), the person who informed Ahasuerus about Haman's gallows was actually Elijah the prophet, who had impersonated Harbona for the occasion! This audacious interpretation may have been suggested by

Rabbi Pinhas's use of the expression "of blessed memory" [*zakhur le-tov*], which is frequently reserved for Elijah.

Even so, when we compare the texts of old prayer books and halakhic compendia, we come to appreciate that they are divided on the question of whether or not to include the blessing for Harbona at the end of the Megillah reading.

In spite of all the ingenious textual tricks that the commentators were able to utilize in support of the midrashic interpretations, my personal suspicion is that Rabbis Hama and Pinhas might have been reading Harbona's personality in the light of their own experiences and values. For reasons that were rooted in his previous encounters with the gentile world, Rabbi Hama may have developed a strong skepticism when it came to friendly gestures by pagans, which led him to denigrate Harbona's contributions to the Jewish cause.

An opinion in the Talmud expresses a similar assessment of another ostensible act of kindness by a non-Jew, in the episode when the insomniac Ahasuerus asks his servants whether Mordecai had ever been rewarded for his service to the king. The servants are quick to point out that Mordecai never received a proper token of royal appreciation.

In connection with this detail, the Talmud quips: "It was not that they loved Mordecai, but rather because they despised Haman" (*Megillah* 16a). Here, too, the commentators scurried to find textual clues that would justify such a negative assessment of ostensibly altruistic behavior. Most of these attempts, like Rabbi Alkabetz's declaration that "it is the normal practice of the righteous to judge the wicked unfavourably," are not quite convincing. Rather than responding to a textual stimulus in the biblical story, I find it more likely that the sages in question were expressing their personal cynicism about the benevolence of heathens.

On the other hand, Rabbi Pinhas appears to have taken a more pragmatic approach to such situations. In his view, one should never be overly dismissive of one's allies, even in cases when their motives are not entirely pure and their support of your cause springs from ulterior considerations. In the end, it is better to have such people in your camp than on the opposite side.

From this perspective, even an opportunistic Harbona should be remembered for good.

Suggestions for Further Reading

Ginzberg, Louis. *The Legends of the Jews*, translated by H. Szold. Philadelphia: Jewish Publication Society of America, 1967.

Grossfeld, Bernard, ed. *The Two Targums of Esther*, edited by M. M. e. al. The Aramaic Bible: The Targums. Collegeville, Minn.: Liturgical Press, 1991.

Jacobson, B. S. *Netiv Binah: Pirqé Mavo, Perushim ve-'Iyunim ba- "Sidur."* Tel-Aviv: Sinai, 1973.

Segal, Eliezer. *The Babylonian Esther Midrash: A Critical Commentary*, 3 vols, Brown Judaic Studies. Atlanta: Scholars Press, 1994.

Passover

The springtime festival of Passover [Hebrew: Pesah] commemorates the miraculous liberation of the ancient Hebrews from centuries of slavery in Egypt. Its most prominent rituals include the eating of matzah (unleavened bread), a strict prohibition of all leavened foods, and the *seder*, the elaborate meal on the first night at which the story of the exodus is told in word and symbol.

Back to Egypt*

I am told that Egypt has now become a popular destination for Jewish Passover tourism. In the present political circumstances, that fashion might be discouraged as foolhardy or ironic. However, previous generations of Jews would have found such a practice problematic for different reasons, primarily because it violates the biblical prohibitions against returning to a land that was once infamous for its idolatrous immorality.

It is nonetheless an undeniable fact that since the days of Moses, Jews have found themselves dwelling in Egypt for a variety of reasons. Thanks to the ancient papyri scattered in the silt of the Nile and the medieval fragments from the Cairo Genizah, we probably possess more complete and continuous documentation of Egyptian Jewry than of any other branch of the tribe.

Among our earliest records is the extraordinary archive of Aramaic documents from the fifth century B.C.E. that was unearthed on the island of Elephantine, near Aswan. On that strategic site overseeing traffic and

* *The Jewish Free Press*, Calgary, March 30, 1999, pp. 22–23.

commerce along the Nile, a garrison of Jewish mercenaries was stationed by the Persian colonial government.

Historians disagree about when the military outpost was first established. Some date it as early as the reign of king Manasseh of Judah in the seventh century B.C.E. It is likely that the community's population was augmented by a later wave of refugees who fled the Babylonian conquest of Judea in 587.

The puzzle of the colony's origins is complicated by a remarkable letter that was preserved, albeit in fragmentary form, in the Elephantine archive. This letter was sent by an individual named Hananiah, apparently from Jerusalem, in "the fifth year of king Darius" (419 B.C.E.).

The tattered document, invoking the authority of the Persian imperial government, informs the addressees, Jedaniah and his colleagues,

> *that they are to keep the festival of Passover on the fourteenth day of Nisan. From the fifteenth until the twenty-first of that month they are to keep the Festival of Unleavened Bread, avoiding work on the first and last days of the holiday, and studiously avoiding the consumption of any leavened products during that period. During those days, any leaven that remains in their possession is to be sealed off in a room.*

Historians have been perplexed by the utter obviousness of the message. Is it conceivable that a Jewish community should have to be officially informed, under governmental auspices, of basic rules of Passover that are set out so clearly in the Torah?

The various attempts to explain this difficulty have generated diverse speculations about its historical context.

Some scholars have indeed drawn the conclusion that the Elephantine Jews had not previously been observing Passover, or at least not in the manner prescribed in the letter.

Several historians have argued that the directive was designed to lay down a uniform date for Passover, in contrast to the diverse practices that existed previously. Perhaps (they suggest) the colonists had hitherto been following an early form of Hebrew religion, according to which the date of Passover was determined by agricultural stages rather than by a fixed date on the calendar. Other scholars speculate that some of the soldiers had been observing Passover according to the Northern Israelite date, which was a month later than that of their Judean cousins.

It is tempting to identify the letter's sender, Hananiah, with his biblical namesake, a relative of Nehemiah who was active in the political affairs of the restored Jerusalem, and may have been appointed Nehemiah's successor. Just as Ezra and Nehemiah had worked hard to impose the authority of the Torah upon the Jewish populations of Jerusalem and the Babylonian diaspora, it is possible that Hananiah was now extending that process to Egyptian Jewry. In fact, it is possible that the main thrust of the letter was to assure the soldiers that they had the full support and encouragement of the Persian government in their observance of the festival.

One topic that seems to have been delicately avoided in the letter was the matter of the paschal offering. According to the normative Jewish policy, which is emphasized most strongly in the Book of Deuteronomy, no sacrifices are permitted outside the Temple in Jerusalem. However, we know that the colonists at Elephantine maintained their own sacrificial temple. This has been taken by some as evidence that the colony was founded before King Josiah adopted the religious reforms that abolished all sacrificial worship outside of Jerusalem.

Though we would expect the Jerusalem leadership to state their condemnation of the illicit sanctuary, Hananiah's letter does not seem to deal at all with that touchy issue, other than by omitting any explicit mention of it. The fragmentary character of the evidence does not allow us to draw firm conclusions on this matter.

At any rate, the matter became moot a few years later, when the Temple at Elephantine was destroyed in a native uprising that took place in 410.

Even after the rebellion was suppressed, order restored, and the perpetrators punished, the Persian authorities were reluctant to authorize the Elephantine temple's rebuilding, and requests for support from the Jerusalem leadership were never answered. In the end, the governor consented to replace the sanctuary only if animal offerings would be forsaken.

The issue that kindled the anger of the Egyptian rebels was more religious than political. In fact, it was a problem that goes back to the roots of the Passover story, to the days of Jacob and Joseph.

Already then, the Israelites were careful not to advertise that they were shepherds because this was considered an offence to the Egyptians. A venerable midrashic tradition makes use of this premise to explain why a lamb was chosen as the Passover sacrifice: It was precisely because sheep were worshipped by the Egyptians; therefore, the Hebrews' fearless preparation and slaughtering of that animal in full view of their pagan neighbours was the ultimate display of their newfound spirit of liberty (*Exodus Rabbah* 16:3).

This was the same situation that existed in the days of the Elephantine sanctuary. Many Egyptians at that time were devoted to the worship of Khnum the ram-god. Hence, in their eyes the Jewish sacrifices of lambs on Passover and on other occasions would have been perceived as an offensive blasphemy, provoking the violent attack that put an end to the Jewish sacrificial cult at Elephantine.

Thus, in true Passover spirit, this colony of Jews who had returned to the soil of Egypt found themselves reliving the same conflicts that their forefathers had experienced in the days of the original exodus.

Suggestions for Further Reading

Ginzberg, Louis. *The Legends of the Jews*, translated by H. Szold. 7 vols. Philadelphia: Jewish Publication Society of America, 1909–39.

Modrzejewski, J. *The Jews of Egypt: From Rameses II to Emperor Hadrian*. Princeton: Princeton University Press, 1997.

Porten, Bezalel. *Archives from Elephantine: the Life of an Ancient Jewish Military Colony*. Berkeley: University of California Press, 1968.

———. "The Calendar of Aramaic Texts from Achaemenid and Ptolemaic Egypt." *Irano-Judaica* 2 (1990): 13–32.

Raphael, Chaim. *A Feast of History: Passover through the Ages as a Key to Jewish Experience*. New York: Simon and Schuster, 1972.

'In Every Generation ...': The Strange Omission in Rabbi Kalischer's Haggadah*

Over the ages, the Passover Haggadah has provided Jewish thinkers with an effective instrument through which to express their most profound thoughts on a variety of religious topics. It was therefore to be expected that when Rabbi Zvi Hirsch Kalischer published his own Haggadah in 1864, it would be filled with original and timely insights about the issues that were of concern to him.

Rabbi Kalischer (1795–1874) was one of the pioneering figures who, decades before Herzl, called upon his fellow Jews to take an active role in creating an independent Jewish society in the land of Israel.

It therefore does not surprise us to discover that his Haggadah included penetrating observations on the contemporary situation, such as this assessment of the political emancipation of European Jewry: "At present, the Almighty has proclaimed liberty for the Jews in most states, and this is a prelude to the time when we shall be free people in the Land of Israel."

* *The Jewish Free Press*, Calgary, March 30, 2000, pp. 14–15.

Similarly, Kalischer's description of how the ancient Hebrew slaves retained their religious distinctiveness served as a contrast to the rampant assimilation that was overtaking many Jews in his own days: "They did not choose to be like the gentiles – like the Egyptians – as one nation, in order to ease their poverty and subjugation, as our contemporaries believe, who wish to be esteemed in the eyes of the gentiles, and are ashamed to observe the Jewish religion." He preached that these manifestations of Jewish self-deprecation would ultimately make them even more despised, and that it was by proudly maintaining their uniqueness that Jews would earn the respect of the nations of the world.

Indeed, Rabbi Kalischer's commentary fulfills all our expectations in serving as a sounding board for his proto-Zionist ideology.

Nevertheless, historians have been troubled by the glaring absence of one theme that had formerly been dear to Kalischer's heart, but which goes virtually unmentioned in his Haggadah in spite of its appropriateness to the context.

The topic is the renewal of sacrificial worship.

As early as 1836, Kalischer had approached Baron de Rothschild urging him to purchase Palestine from the Turkish emperor for purposes of Jewish colonization. At that time Kalischer insisted that, even if the entire homeland could not be acquired, the Baron should at the very least gain possession of the Temple site so that sacrifices might be offered as soon as possible.

In Kalischer's messianic scenario, the resumption of the sacrificial cult must occur at the earliest stages of the process, so that atonement could be obtained for the sins of the people, an essential prerequisite for the subsequent stages in the redemptive process.

Kalischer made it clear that the sacrifices he was speaking of would precede the actual rebuilding of the Temple. He discussed the details of these controversial opinions with some of the leading rabbinic authorities of the time, posing his initial halakhic question to his own teacher Rabbi Akiva Eiger of Posen, who responded quite disapprovingly.

Eiger subsequently turned the matter over to his son-in-law, the renowned Rabbi Moses Schreiber (the "Chasam Sofer") of Pressburg. While assenting in principle to the legality of Kalischer's proposal, the latter noted, with a sense of realism lacking in the young Kalischer, that the Muslims were unlikely to consent to the construction of a Jewish Temple on the site of their mosque.

The Chasam Sofer also noted, citing a previous discussion by Rabbi Jacob Emden of Altona, that according to Jewish law the only sacrifice that could be offered prior to the construction of the Temple, and while the majority of the people were still in a state of impurity, was the Passover offering.

Rabbi Schreiber's statement was not published until several years later, in a book by his student Rabbi Zvi Hirsch Chajes, in which Chajes added his own arguments for the legitimacy of restoring sacrifices. Among other things he noted that, according to the Talmud, sacrifices continued to be offered for about eighty years after the destruction of the Temple.

In 1857, rumours were circulating in the Hebrew press that the Jews in Jerusalem were preparing to offer the Passover offering, in accordance with Rabbi Kalischer's ruling.

This inspired a spirited correspondence between several of Europe's foremost scholars and rabbinical figures. Those who opposed Kalischer's ideas (including the historian Heinrich Graetz) cited Maimonides' ruling that prayer was not merely a replacement for sacrifices, but an evolutionary step beyond it.

And yet, for all his early enthusiasm for the renewal of sacrifices, Rabbi Kalischer's commentary on the Passover Haggadah, which seemed like the ideal vehicle for advocating this idea, tacitly abandoned the call for immediate renewal of the sacrifices, replacing it with discussions about political emancipation and national liberation. Though the text of the Haggadah provided him with a perfect opening when it prayed for the time when "we shall eat of the sacrifices and the Passover offerings," Rabbi Kalischer did not exploit the opportunity to argue for his youthful dream.

Evidently, the key to this inconsistency may be found in the extensive changes that European Jewry had undergone in the intervening decades.

At the beginning of the century, Jewish traditionalists were up in arms over radical attempts at liturgical reform, such as the notorious 1819 Hamburg prayer book that had deleted references to sacrificial worship and the return to Zion. These time-honoured Jewish values were judged by the champions of religious reform to be at odds with their aspirations to be accepted as enlightened, patriotic European citizens "of the Mosaic faith." The traditionalist forces fought a lengthy campaign to ban the publication of the new-style prayer books.

At that time, responding to these challenges, Kalischer deemed it important to promote traditional Jewish values and aspirations, and it made perfect sense to present the renewal of sacrifices as an indispensable prerequisite of Messianic redemption. With very few exceptions (including Rabbi Akiva Eiger), the views that had been voiced for and against Kalischer's proposal had been split precisely along ideological lines, between the traditionalists and the reformers.

However, thirty years later, when he published his Haggadah commentary, the situation had changed considerably. For one thing, his ideas about sacrifices had proven very unpopular, even among individuals who were in other respects supportive of his program.

More importantly, there were now more urgent matters on the public agenda. The Jews in the Holy Land were in dire economic distress in the aftermath of the Crimean War. The European emancipation was a *fait accompli*, and the pressing need for political action and economic self-sufficiency took priority over issues that had seemed so important thirty years earlier. Furthermore, the reports (untrue, as it happens) that the Jews of the Holy City were on the verge of actively offering sacrifices caused alarm among rabbis who had hitherto been dealing with the matter on a comfortable theoretical level and as part of their anti-Reform polemic; but who generally shied away from messianic enthusiasm. A newer generation of Orthodox and Neo-Orthodox rabbis in Germany, including Jacob Ettlinger and Samson Raphael Hirsch, shared many of the modernist assumptions about the superiority of prayer over animal sacrifice. Therefore, the tide of halakhic opinion now turned solidly against Kalischer.

The Haggadah instructs us that in each generation we ought to see ourselves as if we had personally experienced the Egyptian Exodus. In the case of Rabbi Kalischer, the pace of social and political changes had accelerated so much that, within a single generation, he was impelled to interpret the lessons of the Haggadah in very different ways.

Suggestions for Further Reading

Bleich, J. David. "A Review of Halakhic Literature Pertaining to the Reinstitution of the Sacrificial Order." *Tradition* 9 (1967): 103–24.

Katz, Jacob. "Demuto ha-historit shel ha-rav zevi hirsch kalischer." *Shivat Zion* 2–3 (1952–53): 26–41.

Salmon, Yosef. "The Rise of Jewish Nationalism on the Border of Eastern and Western Europe: Rabbi Z. H. Kalischer, David Gordon, Peretz Smolenskin." In *Danzig, East and West: Aspects of Modern Jewish History*, edited by I. Twersky. Cambrdge: Harvard Center for Jewish Studies and Harvard Semitic Museum, 1985.

Ticker, Jay. *The Centrality of Sacrifices as an Answer to Reform in the Thought of Zvi Hirsch Kalischer.* Vol. 15, *Working Papers in Yiddish and East European Studies. New York: YIVO, 1975.*

The Eggs and the Exodus*

More than any other festival in the Jewish calendar, Passover is defined by its foods. The basic obligations to eat matzah and bitter herbs, as well as the obligation to remove all leaven from one's home, are explicitly commanded by the Torah as memorials to the slavery of Egypt and the miraculous deliverance from oppression. A glance at the foods on the traditional seder plate immediately evokes the immense volumes of history, values, and emotions that are associated with the themes of the holiday.

Amidst this wealth of solemn symbolism lies one humble foodstuff whose significance is less than obvious, and whose function in the seder is so obscure that it is likely to remain on the table until the end of the meal without ever getting eaten, or even mentioned.

I am referring to the lowly Passover egg.

The Torah does not command us to eat an egg, or to stare at one during the Passover meal. The egg is mentioned briefly in the Talmud as part of the festive menu,

---

**The Jewish Free Press*, Calgary, April 20, 2000, pp. 22–23.

but without attaching any distinctive value to it, let alone ordaining a place of honour for it on the seder plate.

Talmudic sources speak of serving "two cooked dishes" at the Passover meal, especially for people who are not partaking of the paschal sacrifice in the Temple. The rabbis offered diverse recommendations as to what these two items ought to be: meat, rice, a bone, beets, fish ... or (according to one opinion among several) an egg (*Pesahim* 114b).

A tradition cited in the Jerusalem Talmud [*Pesahim* 10:3 (37d)] states that the requirement to eat two dishes has a symbolic meaning beyond the mere enhancement of the feast: "One dish is a memorial of the Passover sacrifice, and the other is a memorial for the pilgrimage offering [*hagigah*]."

In the Babylonian Talmud this symbolism was attached only to meat dishes (*Pesahim* 114b). Neither Talmud indicated that eggs had any relevance in this connection.

However, as we proceed through history we observe a subtle, though persistent, tendency to bestow upon the egg a ritual status of its own in the context of the *seder.*

A responsum ascribed to Rav Sherira Ga'on, who presided over the Babylonian academy of Pumbedita during the tenth century, explained the need for two foods in a different way: "They commemorate the two messengers, Moses and Aaron, whom the Almighty sent to Egypt." And in the interests of egalitarianism he is careful to note that "some serve an additional dish in order to commemorate Miriam, as it says (Micah 6:4) 'and I sent before thee Moses, Aaron, and Miriam.'"

The three foods that Rav Sherira recommends are: fish, meat and ... an egg. And aside from their association with the three shepherds of Israel, Rav Sherira describes yet another significance. They correspond to the three foods upon which Israel will feast in the Next World; namely: fish, corresponding to the Leviathan; the egg, corresponding to the wondrous bird known as *ziz saddai* [see Psalms 50:11; 80:14]; and meat, corresponding to the wild ox.

Thus, our unassuming Passover egg has now taken on eschatological dimensions, representing one of the menu items in that great banquet that the righteous will enjoy in the messianic epoch.

Rabbinic tradition identified the *ziz saddai* as a fabulous bird, so enormous that when it spreads it wings it eclipses the sun (*Bava Batera* 73b). Furthermore, the flesh of the *ziz* comes in many different flavours, all of them kosher. Its presence at the messianic feast will more than compensate for all the non-kosher birds that Jews have refrained from enjoying in deference to the divine commandments.

The customs that evolved among the Jews of Italy tried to accommodate all the different symbolisms by placing on the seder table two kinds of meat (roast and boiled) to represent the Passover and pilgrimage offerings; as well as the fish and egg that commemorate the messianic repast.

The Italians were just about the only medieval community in which the egg had a quasi-official status at the seder. Most of the halakhic authorities did not stipulate specific foods. Those who did, like Maimonides, insisted on two meat dishes.

Among more recent interpreters the view has taken hold that the meat at the table is intended to represent the Passover sacrifice, while the egg symbolizes the pilgrimage sacrifice. This notion is a departure from the earlier and more logical view that used meat to symbolize both sacrifices. The commentators were hard put to find any meaningful connection between an egg and an animal offering.

Rabbi Aaron of Lunel, the author of an important compendium on Jewish customs, pointed out that eggs, because they represent the circularity of life and death, are traditionally served to mourners; and he suggested accordingly that their role on Passover is also to express our sorrow over the destruction of the Temple and our inability to offer sacrifices there. Rabbi Moses Isserles found support for this motif in a peculiarity of the Hebrew calendar that has the first night of Passover always fall on the same day of the week as the Ninth of Av, the anniversary of the destruction of the two Temples.

Other authorities opposed this interpretation on the grounds that it is inappropriate to mourn during a festival. For this reason, Rabbi Moses Feinstein discouraged the eating of eggs at the seder.

Truly, the tenacity with which our egg has insinuated itself into the Passover ceremony seems unrelated to any of the symbolic or halakhic explanations that have been proposed for its presence. When confronted by such anomalies, scholars are strongly tempted to ascribe the phenomena to foreign influences.

An obvious suspect would be the Christian practice of handing out coloured eggs in connection with the Easter holiday, which occurs at the same season of the year. To be precise, the Easter egg itself is a curious holdover from pre-Christian fertility celebrations that survived in popular European custom.

It is, of course, out of the question to accuse our pious forefathers of imitating such a blatantly un-Jewish practice. And furthermore, there is a considerable leap between the simple Passover egg and the coloured ones that are left by the Easter bunny.

And yet, to be honest, there were localities in Poland where it was customary for Jews to "go for a *vikup*" during Passover. The practice (the Yiddish expression is related to a Polish word meaning "ransom") involved paying a visit to relatives and receiving from them coloured eggs, especially ones that were tinted yellowish-red with the help of a special formula extracted from onion skins.

In some Hasidic circles, including the Karlin and Lubavitch sects, the distribution of painted eggs took place later in the season, on Lag Ba-'omer.

A children's magazine published by Chabad-Lubavitch in 1945 described the thrill of a group of children as they prepared for the festivities. One of the children was especially excited because "Mommy promised to prepare some hard-boiled eggs for my Lag

B'Omer lunch – *coloured.*" When asked about the reason for this practice, she explained that the eggs are an expression of mourning for the death of Rabbi Simeon ben Yohai, which occurred on that date. However, Rabbi Simeon

> *was very happy when the time came to surrender his soul to the Creator, because he knew that everlasting happiness awaited him. And so, while the Lag B'Omer eggs are to remind us of his death, their purpose is not to make us feel sad on this day. Lag B'Omer is a children's festival, and children love color. And so it became customary to paint the shells of the eggs in various colors to make the children feel very happy on Lag B'Omer.*

It was not only in Europe that Jews were drawn to coloured eggs. In Afghanistan, the eggs made their ritual appearance earlier in the season and were associated with the Purim festivities. Throughout the month of Adar it was the custom there to hold egg-rolling contests, to see whose could keep going the longest without breaking. For each egg that did get crushed in the competition, the children would curse Haman. In Kurdistan, coloured eggs were included in the *Mishloah manot* that were distributed to children on Purim.

It would appear that the persistence of the eggs in the Jewish springtime festivities might have had its roots in borrowings from cross-cultural folklore.

Or are we perhaps dealing with an ancient Hebrew springtime custom that somehow avoided being mentioned in any of the official sources?

It sounds like one of those eternal chicken-or-egg questions.

Suggestions for Further Reading

Brauer, Erich, and Raphael Patai. *The Jews of Kurdistan*, edited by R. Patai. *Jewish Folklore and Anthropology Series*. Detroit: Wayne State University Press, 1993.

Goldberg, Harvey E. "Anthropology and the Study of Traditional Jewish Societies." *AJS Review* 15(1) (1990): 1–22.

Herzog, Marvin. *The Yiddish Language in Northern Poland: Its Geography and History, Indiana University Research Center in Anthropology, Folklore and Linguistics*. Bloomington and The Hague: University of Indiana Press and Mouton, 1965.

Merkos L'Inyonei Chinuch. "Lag B'Omer," *Shaloh (Shi'urei Limmud Ve-das)*, May 1, 1945, 1–4.

Mondshein, Joshua, ed. *Otsar Minhagei Haba"d*, 2 vols. Jerusalem: Heikhal Manahem, 1996.

Tabory, Yosef. *The Passover Ritual Through the Generations*, edited by M. Ayali. *Hillel ben Hayyim Library*. Tel-Aviv: Hakibbutz Hameuchad Publishing House, 1996 [Hebrew].

Dressing for Success*

The midrash teaches us that in their long years of slavery in Egypt, our Hebrew ancestors retained very little of the national identity that had been defined by the Patriarchs and Matriarchs. When the time came for their redemption, the spiritual flame had been all but extinguished by their dehumanizing labours.

And yet, the rabbis found clues that some traces of the sacred Jewish spark still burned in their hearts and minds. In several passages in the midrash, they listed qualities by virtue of which the Israelites were found worthy of redemption.

The virtues that are mentioned in this connection include the following: They were not suspected of sexual impropriety, and therefore their pedigrees were beyond reproach. They did not gossip or betray secrets, including the divine assurance that they possessed of their eventual redemption. They kept their Hebrew names. They continued to speak the Hebrew language (see *Leviticus Rabbah* 32:5; *Pesiqta de-Rav Kahana* 11:7; etc.). Even

* *The Jewish Free Press*, Calgary, March 2, 2001, pp. 12–13.

though most of these qualities were matters of ethnic solidarity rather than moral or spiritual achievements, they were the necessary condition for their survival as a holy people.

One of the most respected nineteenth-century experts on midrashic literature was Solomon Buber, the grandfather of Martin. This Galician savant, who was also a prominent businessman, scoured the libraries of Europe for Hebrew manuscripts, from which he published dozens of ancient rabbinic midrashim, each of which he supplemented with erudite scholarly annotations and introductions that testify to his encyclopedic knowledge of Hebrew and classical literature.

Hidden away among his copious footnotes to one of those texts is a brief comment concerning the tradition about the virtues of the ancient Hebrews: "However, the widely quoted saying 'and they did not change their garb' is not found anywhere.'"

After pausing briefly to wonder at Buber's ability – unassisted by concordances or CD-ROMs – to make such a categorical pronouncement that something is *not* found in the vast sea of rabbinic literature, we might take note of the peculiarity of his comment. What indeed is the point of discussing a non-existent source? And how did a non-existent source come into circulation among Buber's contemporaries?

Buber himself noted that the misquote about the Hebrews not changing their garb had an earlier history. He mentions that it is to be found in the writings of the celebrated philologist and author Elijah Levita (c. 1468–

1549). The German-born Levita spent most of his career in Italy, where he taught Hebrew language and literature to Christian Humanists. Although he remained loyal to Jewish tradition, several of his descendants converted to Christianity and even assisted the church's attacks on the Talmud and other Jewish religious works.

Another prominent scholar who had "misquoted" the midrash was Rabbi Yom-Tov ben Abraham Ishbili (known by his acronym "Ritva"), one of the foremost talmudic commentators of 13th–14th century Spain. Unlike several of his teachers, the Ritva was an enthusiastic supporter of general scientific and philosophical studies, and composed a work in defence of Maimonides.

The misquote also appears in an eleventh-century midrashic compilation called *Lekah Tov* composed in Bulgaria by Rabbi Tobiah ben Eliezer. At that time, Bulgaria held liberal attitudes towards Jews and Judaism, and the Orthodox church had adopted a favourable attitude towards its Jewish roots. One of Rabbi Tobiah's students, Leo Mung, later achieved distinction as Archbishop and Primate of Bulgaria.

In his commentary to the Passover Haggadah, Don Isaac Abravanel also embellished the rabbinic tradition, stating that the ancient Hebrews did not change their language, their names, their garb, or their religion. Abravanel, of course, was another figure with strong connections to the host society. He was a statesman and financier who served as treasury minister under Ferdinand and Isabella until the expulsions from Spain and

Portugal, and he subsequently continued his diplomatic activities in Naples and Venice.

Thus, the statement about the Hebrews not changing their garb seems to surface under consistently similar circumstances: in societies where the lines between Jew and gentile were very flexible, and where it was possible to cross those lines with relative ease. It was in such a historical context that Jewish religious leaders became especially conscious of the need to maintain visible indications of their distinctiveness. Even so, the earliest texts that cite this tradition about special Jewish clothing explain it with references to specific religious laws, especially the requirement to wear ritual *tzitzit*. They do not seem to have in mind a peculiarly Jewish style of dress.

In several respects, the situation in which Solomon Buber lived was similar to the ones that had been faced by those earlier rabbis. From the beginnings of the European Jewish Emancipation, especially after the time of Napoleon, the Jews of central and eastern Europe were subjected to strong pressure to assimilate to the majority ethos. These pressures usually included official edicts against the wearing of traditional Jewish attire. The promise of civil rights was held out to the Jews, but it was often made conditional upon relinquishing their distinctive dress.

Buber himself stood at the crossroads of these conflicting movements. He was equally at home in the traditional Judaism of Poland and Russia (it was he who kindled his grandson Martin's fascination with Hasidism) and in modern European society and general culture (as may be learned from the ease with which he cites Greek and Latin sources in his commentaries to midrashic texts). It is likely that the popularization of the statement about the Hebrews' not changing their garb originated among the Hasidim, whose well-known commitment to distinctive Jewish clothing served as an effective defence against the inroads of alien culture.

No one knew better than the sages of the Talmud that you should not look at the container, but at the contents (*Avot* 4:20). Nevertheless, there are times when people's choices of attire speak volumes about their values and self-image.

Evidently some people believed that this truth is so momentous that if it is not actually found in the midrash, then it ought to be.

Suggestions for Further Reading

Buber, Solomon, ed. *Pesiqta de-Rav Kahana*, Lyck: L. Silvermann, 1868.

Eisenbach, Artur. *The Emancipation of the Jews in Poland, 1780–1870*, translated by J. Dorosz, edited by D. Sorkin. *Jewish Society and Culture*. Oxford: Basil Blackwell in association with the Institute for Jewish Studies, 1991.

Kasher, Menahem. *Torah Shelemah (Complete Torah): Encyclopedia of the Pentateuch*. New York: American Biblical Encyclopedia Society, 1927–81 [Hebrew].

Hillel's Perplexing Passover Predicament*

The Jewish religious leadership was facing a baffling quandary. The pilgrims had gathered for Passover, eager to partake in the festival sacrifice. This was a celebration that had been observed in the Jerusalem Temple every spring for hundreds of years. And yet on this occasion, the community seemed paralyzed by indecision.

What made this particular Passover different was the fact that it began on a Saturday night. In normal years, when the holiday followed directly upon a weekday, the preparation of the lamb for the *seder* was a relatively straightforward matter. However, this year no one seemed certain how to deal with the Torah's severe restrictions against cooking, slaughtering, kindling, and other activities that were required for the preparations, but were normally prohibited as violations of the Sabbath. The elders of Beteira, who held the position of leadership at the time, were unable to arrive at a solution (*Pesahim* 66a).

* *The Jewish Free Press*, Calgary, April 5, 2001, pp 20–21.

Someone informed the elders, with no small measure of skepticism, about a certain immigrant, recently arrived from Babylonia, who claimed to have the answer. This unknown newcomer, Hillel by name, claimed to have studied with the foremost teachers of the previous generation. Desperate to resolve the issue, the elders reluctantly consented to hear him out.

In a dazzling display of scholarly erudition, Hillel began to heap proof upon proof to show that the preparation of the sacrifice overrides the Sabbath prohibitions. He pointed out that the daily *Tamid* offerings in the Temple were burned even on Saturdays, as were the Additional (*Musaf*) offerings of the Sabbath or of any festival that happened to occur on the Sabbath. Hillel went on to argue that the Passover had an even greater claim to supersede the Sabbath restrictions, since failure to bring its sacrifice carried with it the severe penalty of *karet,* premature death by divine agency. Hillel also pointed out that the Torah itself (Numbers 9:2) had placed special stress on the obligation to "keep the Passover at its *appointed time*" – thereby indicating that it should not be cancelled or rescheduled.

The above story was recorded in several different versions in talmudic literature [see *Tosefta Pesahim* 4:11; Jerusalem Talmud *Pesahim* 6:1 (33a)], and it is generally regarded as a milestone in the history of Jewish tradition. The development of Judaism from the beginnings of the Second Temple until Hillel's time is shrouded in obscurity, and only a handful of sages from that era have survived in rabbinic memory. It is with Hillel that we begin the new age of intensive scholarly activity that will culminate in the publication of the Mishnah and the Talmuds.

In this report about how Hillel proved that the Passover sacrifice overrides the Sabbath, we find the earliest mention of systematic methods for deriving new teachings from biblical texts. These methods, known as Midrash, would afterwards become defining features of Jewish religious discourse.

Interestingly, the Jerusalem Talmud reports that Hillel's audience was not all that impressed by his scholarly pyrotechnics. They were able to refute all his logical and textual proofs, and concluded dismissively that his performance only reinforced the low expectations they had from a Babylonian greenhorn.

In the end, Hillel had to appeal to traditional authority, asserting that he had received his ruling from his eminent teachers, Shemayah and Avtalion. It was this reliance on tradition that eventually clinched the matter, and led to Hillel's immediate appointment to the position of *Nasi*, the head of the academy.

One problem that troubled the later rabbis as they pondered this story was the question of how it was possible that, among the thousands of Passover pilgrims who had assembled for the holiday, there could not be found a single person who remembered what had been done the last time Passover followed Shabbat. Although such occurrences are relatively infrequent (there were, for example, none between 1994 and 2001), *somebody* must have recalled how they had dealt with the situation the last time it happened.

The Talmud ascribes this enigma to supernatural intervention: God *caused* the people to forget in order to make Hillel's achievement appear more impressive and to facilitate his rapid rise to leadership.

Recent developments in history and archaeology suggest some other ways to explain the circumstances of Hillel's pronouncement about what to do when Passover falls after Shabbat.

A very interesting point of comparison is provided by the Dead Sea Scrolls, many of which were composed close to Hillel's lifetime. The scrolls, evidently authored by followers of the Essene sect, advocate a very different calendar from the one currently followed by mainstream Judaism. In their 364-day solar calendar, holidays fall on the same day of the week every year. Passover can occur only on Wednesday, rendering Hillel's problem an impossibility.

We have seen that Hillel's Babylonian origins were alluded to repeatedly in the talmudic accounts, usually in a sarcastic or demeaning way. In fact, our 354-day lunar calendric cycle is virtually identical to the ancient Babylonian system. It therefore makes sense that opponents of our Pharisaic-rabbinic method of time-reckoning would try to emphasize Hillel's foreign origins, as a way of ridiculing the calendar that he advocated.

It should be noted as well that Dead Sea religious law generally tried to avoid conflicts or incompatibilities between different commandments. In this respect, they differed from the talmudic sages, who derived special intellectual satisfaction from devising unlikely cases in which they would have to sort out conflicting legal priorities. Thus, to take one example, Hillel's reliance on the precedent of the *Tamid* offering, in order to deduce that the Passover lamb is prepared even on the Sabbath, would have made no sense to an Essene, since their system did not allow the *Tamid* to be offered on Shabbat in the first place.

It is possible, therefore, that the rare occurrence of Passover on a Saturday night, and the halakhic complications that it occasioned, were seized upon by champions of the Dead Sea calendar as effective propaganda against the calendar system followed by the majority of Jews.

If this hypothesis is correct, then the problem dealt with by Hillel takes on much greater significance. It was not simply a matter of a memory lapse, or even of deciding between two opposing legal priorities. What might have taken place was a major confrontation between two Jewish sects, each representing a distinct attitude towards religious authority, scriptural interpretation, and spiritual values. Hillel was being called upon to defend the coherence of the Pharisaic oral tradition by demonstrating that it was based on an intelligent reading of the relevant verses from the Torah.

Although this reconstruction of the event is purely speculative, it accounts for several of the most mystifying details in the story.

Above all, it provides a more satisfying explanation as to why Hillel's achievement was considered so important that it led to his installation as *Nasi* of Israel. In the end, in arguing that the Passover lamb could be prepared on the Sabbath, Hillel was acting as an eloquent spokesman for the entire Jewish ancestral tradition.

A century or so after this fateful confrontation, the Jerusalem Temple lay in ruins and the sacrifices could not be offered. Neither the Sadducees nor the Essenes were able to adapt to the new reality, and neither group was heard from again.

However, the Pharisees did survive; and their successors, the talmudic rabbis, succeeded in adapting Jewish tradition to the changing times.

The fact that they were able to do so was due in no small part to the solid foundations that had been laid by a Babylonian Jewish immigrant named Hillel.

Suggestions for Further Reading

Glatzer, Nahum Norbert. *Hillel the Elder: The Emergence of Classical Judaism*. Rev. ed. A Hillel book. New York: Schocken Books, 1966.

Lieberman, Saul. *Hellenism in Jewish Palestine: Studies in the Literary Transmission, Beliefs, and Manners of Palestine in the I century B.C.E. – IV century C.E.* 2nd improved ed. *Texts and Studies of the Jewish Theological Seminary of America*. New York: Jewish Theological Seminary of America, 1962.

Schiffman, Lawrence H. *The Halakhah at Qumran*, edited by J. Neusner. Studies in Judaism in Late Antiquity. Leiden: Brill, 1975.

Old King, New King*

The beginning of the Hebrew enslavement in Egypt, as recounted in the opening chapters of the Book of Exodus, was occasioned by the ascension to the throne of "a new king over Egypt, who knew not Joseph" (Exodus 1:8).

The meaning of this verse was debated by Jewish sages in third-century Babylonia (*Eruvin* 53a; *Sotah* 11a).

According to one opinion, the verse is to be accepted at face value as indicating that the old Pharaoh who had befriended Joseph and extended hospitality to his family was now deceased, and was succeeded by a different ruler who instituted malevolent policies towards his Hebrew subjects.

However, others advocated a very different reading of the situation: The evil Pharaoh was the same individual as before. What was "new" was not his identity, but his attitude. In other words, the selfsame monarch who had elevated Joseph to greatness subsequently underwent a change of heart and issued new decrees against the children of Israel. According to this view, the Torah's

* *The Jewish Free Press*, Calgary, March 14, 2002, pp. 8–9.

assertion that Pharaoh "knew not Joseph" alludes to a self-imposed amnesia about Egypt's debt to their Hebrew benefactor.

The Talmud, in order to defend this strained reading of the biblical text, observes that the Torah makes no explicit mention of the death of a Pharaoh. According to the peculiar midrashic modes of reading sacred texts, this kind of argument from silence may be viewed as evidence that the original Pharaoh was still alive and reigning when the Israelites were reduced to slavery.

The Jewish sages have often allowed themselves to take liberties with the literal meaning of the Bible in order to elicit new insights and moral guidance. In the present instance, however, generations of commentators have struggled to understand what lesson is learned from what appears to be a contrived manipulation of the scriptural passage.

I believe that a better understanding of the talmudic discussion might be achieved if we bear in mind some of the literary and rhetorical features that govern midrashic discourse.

Much of the literature that is included in ancient midrashic collections originated in the sermons that were preached in ancient synagogues. Midrashic interpretations were normally built around confrontations between verses from different parts of the Bible. In this manner, the rabbis were able to reinforce the fundamental unity of sacred scripture and also suggest novel possibilities of interpretation.

This is the same attitude that underlies our practice of matching the Torah readings on Sabbaths and festivals with *haftarot* from the Prophets section of the Bible. Indeed, the interplay between the *haftarah* and the Torah reading provided inspiration for many expositions in talmudic and midrashic literature.

A survey of midrashic collections reveals that several discourses for the opening section of Exodus were based on expositions of Hosea 5:7, which contains a scathing condemnation of Israel: "They have dealt treacherously against the Lord: for they have begotten strange children, now shall a month devour them with their portions."

The allusion to being devoured by a "month" is exceptionally obscure, and scholars continue to argue about its correct interpretation.

The midrashic preachers stressed the etymological relationship between the Hebrew word *hodesh* (translated here in its usual sense of "month") and its basic root meaning of "new." This inspired them to formulate elaborate sermons in which the enslavement of the Israelites in Egypt was blamed on their readiness to introduce innovations into their ancestral traditions.

The ancient sermons identified specific practices that they viewed as symptomatic of the Israelites' assimilation to Egyptian lifestyles. Singled out for special denunciation was the practice of some Hebrews of neglecting to circumcise their children, or even of undergoing surgical procedures to undo their own circumcisions (*Tanhuma Shemot* 5; *Exodus Rabbah* 1:8).

Another "new" practice for which the Israelites were censured was their adoption of the foreign hairstyle known as the *b'lurit,* which provided further proof of their affection for gentile lifestyles, and might even involve participation in heathen religious rituals, since the Greeks and Romans would sometimes clip their *b'lurits* and offer them to assorted spirits or deities.

Thus, by reading the Exodus story and the Hosea verse in counterpoint, the rabbis were able to conclude that it was on account of their adoption of new and untraditional practices that the generation of Israelites following Joseph's death had "begotten strange children," and it was this offence of "newness" that led ultimately to their being "devoured" by Pharaoh's new decrees.

As is to be expected of any worthwhile sermon, the preachers' concern was not so much with the shortcomings of their long-dead ancestors as with the behaviour of their own contemporaries. Under Roman rule, it was convenient for some individuals to keep their Jewishness under wraps. In times of official anti-Jewish persecutions (such as those associated with the Bar Kokhba uprising in 135 C.E.), the practice of circumcision might even have been a legally punishable offence under Roman law.

The midrashic preachers warned their congregations of the gravity of these dangers by projecting them back to the days of Joseph and Moses. The message was now unmistakable: Just as in days of yore the injection of new and foreign elements into the tradition brought about a sudden and fatal transformation of the Israelites' idyllic status in Egypt, so too in the present time, any compromising of Jewish norms will lead to catastrophic consequences.

Another possible link between the enslavement of the Hebrews and the concept of "newness" is furnished by Exodus 12:1–20, which begins "This month shall be unto you the beginning of months [*hodashim*]," again using the same lexical root that designates both "month" and "new." This passage, which is read on the Sabbath preceding the New Moon of Nissan, serves as a liturgical prologue to Passover, and would have provided a convenient opportunity for preachers to dwell upon the evils of religious innovations and their fatal consequences for the children of Israel.

Seen from this perspective, we might be able to suggest a more cogent explanation for the talmudic debate over the identity of the new Pharaoh.

The rabbi who emphasized the newness of the *decrees*, rather than of the *king*, was really trying to stress that the change of circumstances was more important than the question of royal succession. Accordingly, the practical lesson to be derived from the Exodus narrative is that, in keeping with the measure-for-measure logic of Jewish history, any unacceptable departure from established tradition will be punished by a deterioration of the condition of the Jews.

To this extent, it is the people themselves who will determine their destiny – and the fate of the Jewish people can be transformed as easily under a single Pharaoh as under two.

These valuable and timeless lessons were made possible by our rabbis' boldness in proposing novel interpretations to familiar biblical texts, allowing the ancient scriptures to remain fresh and new for each generation.

Suggestions for Further Reading

Heinemann, Joseph, and Jakob Josef Petuchowski. *Literature of the Synagogue, Library of Jewish Studies*. New York: Behrman House, 1975.

Drip before You Sip*

There comes a time during the course of the Passover seder when some of us are inclined to take an admiring look at the sparkling white tablecloth, radiant with beautiful festival dishes and fancy silverware.

And then we cringe.

The occasion for this uneasiness is the anticipation of a picturesque custom in which we begin to trickle droplets of wine from our cups.

Ideally, the dripping should be contained safely in a plate or other designated vessel. In the real world, however, you can be certain that at least some of the wine will end up being soaked into the tablecloth, while remnants will remain on the children's fingers for future smearing into the walls or holiday clothing.

This is, of course, one of those little inconveniences that we are happy to put up with for the sake of a meaningful celebration of the festival of freedom.

According to the familiar practice, the spilling of the wine commences with the quotation from the prophet

---

* *The Jewish Free Press*, Calgary, March 28, 2002, pp. 8–9.

Joel (2:30): "And I will show wonders in the heavens and in the earth, *blood,* and *fire,* and *pillars of smoke.*" A dripping is performed for each of the three wonders that were mentioned in the verse, and then again with the enumeration of each of the ten plagues inflicted upon Egypt.

The matter does not stop there, as yet another three wine drops are spilled to correspond to the three-word mnemonic abbreviations proposed by Rabbi Judah to remember the correct order of the plagues: *D'tzakh, 'Adash, Be'ahav.*

As several medieval commentators point out, the total number of drippings was considered crucial. The fact that they added up to sixteen was invested with allegoric or mystical importance, especially in the writings of the German pietists of the *Hasidei Ashkenaz* movement, who often channelled their spiritual energies to counting the numerological values of the letters or the numbers of words in prayers and sacred texts.

Some interpreters stated that the number of the wine drops corresponded to the sixteen blades of a terrifying sword wielded by the Angel of Death. Thus, in splattering the wine outside the cup, we are trying to assure ourselves that death will remain on the *outside.*

In the name of Rabbi Eleazar Rokeah, it was pointed out that this same number sixteen underlies some central Jewish observances, such as the numbers of lambs offered in the Temple during a normal week; or of men called to the reading of the Torah during the week (seven on Saturday morning, and three each on Saturday afternoon and Monday and Thursday mornings).

And if anybody feels skeptical about such bizarre associations, Rabbi Rokeah is quick to admonish them: "You should not scoff at the customs of our holy ancestors."

Rabbi Jacob Moelin (the Maharil) offered his own version of the reasoning behind the practice: Since the cup of wine is traditionally associated with blessings, it follows that spilling the drops outside the cup can transfer destructive plagues away from Israel, and deflect them onto our persecutors. The anonymous commentary printed in the Prague Haggadah links this sentiment to the biblical text (Exodus 15:26) "I will put none of these diseases upon thee, which I have brought upon the Egyptians."

Most of the interpretations that we have cited here have a vengeful or vindictive tone to them, in that they are concerned with metaphorically diverting the plagues away from Israel and towards the Egyptians or their latter-day successors. This xenophobia reflects the historical origins of the custom in medieval German communities, where relations with the Christian majority were often strained, and Passover could serve as the occasion for anti-Jewish violence.

A more enlightened attitude may be evident in the Sepharadic milieu, in a quotation ascribed to Don Isaac Abravanel's commentary to the Passover Haggadah. Although he himself was a victim of the Spanish and Portuguese expulsions, it was reported that Abravanel's exegesis expressed the universalistic sentiment that our cup of joy cannot be full as long as our liberation has to involve punishment of others.

A similar interpretation was favoured by Rabbi Samson Raphael Hirsch and other nineteenth-century scholars. In fact, this last-mentioned rationale has became the most frequently cited one at North American seders, and I have found that the older medieval explanations are virtually unknown to most modern Jews.

Some interesting divergences of opinion surround the proper manner in which the wine should be dripped. Each tiny detail in the procedure was felt to be fraught with symbolic meaning, and therefore could not be left to the discretion of individuals.

Thus, Rabbi Moses Isserles insisted that the wine should be spilled by placing the forefinger in the cup. It is this limb that in Hebrew is referred to as *esba*, the generic word for "finger," and it therefore evokes the biblical passage in which Pharaoh's magicians declared that "This is the finger of God" (Exodus 8:15). On these grounds, Isserles rejects the widespread custom of performing the ritual with the pinkie.

A different procedure was recommended by the great Kabbalistic master Rabbi Isaac Luria of Safed. He was opposed to the whole notion of dripping with fingertips, and insisted that the sixteen drops be poured directly from the cup. Other Kabbalistic teachers added that the liquid should be discharged into a broken vessel, a variation that has profound allegorical importance in Jewish mystical lore.

Another difference of opinion arose concerning the desirability of drinking the wine that remains after the drops have been removed. Rabbi Hayyim Vital reports that some celebrants were careful to rinse out the cup and avoided partaking of a beverage that had been associated with deadly plagues.

Other authorities, however, were quick to point out that it was the sixteen drops that had negative associations, and these had, after all, been removed. The remaining wine, for this reason, should be considered particularly wholesome and salutary.

And indeed, there were Jews who believed that there was exceptional virtue attached to the act of sipping the wine left over from the "plague drops." Drinking this potion was considered an effective charm for guaranteeing a prosperous year.

For a promise of such abundant blessings, it might even be worth risking a few wine stains on your Passover tablecloth.

Suggestions for Further Reading

Fox, Shlomo, and Yisrael Isser Zvi Herczeg, eds. *The Passover Haggadah with the Commentary of Don Isaac Abarbanel.* 1st ed. *ArtScroll Mesorah Series.* Brooklyn, NY: Mesorah Publications, 1990.

Glatzer, Nahum Norbert. *The Passover Haggadah.* 3rd revised ed. New York: Schocken Books, 1979.

Kasher, Menachem M. *Hagadah Shelemah: The Complete Passover Hagadah.* 3rd ed. Jerusalem: Torah Shelema Institute, 1967 [Hebrew].

Katzenellenbogen, Mordecai Leib. *Hagadah Shel Pesah Torat Hayim.* Jerusalem: Mosad ha-Rav Kook, 1998.

Raphael, Chaim. *A Feast of History: Passover through the Ages as a Key to Jewish Experience.* New York: Simon and Schuster, 1972.

Roth, Cecil. *The Haggadah: A New Edition.* London: Soncino Press, 1934.

Those Magnificent Men and Their Matzah Machines*

What an efficient piece of work is a box of matzahs! With its compact brick-like shape, it can be easily transported and stacked on supermarket shelves; and it provides a convenient means for kosher travellers to maintain a minimum diet while venturing into ritually challenged frontiers.

Not so those expensive hand-baked matzahs that we purchase for the *seder.* With their unwieldy shapes, they have to be individually wrapped and packaged as if they were delicate crystal; and even so, special blessings are still advised in order to ensure that they arrive intact, and not as a jumble of disconnected crumbs.

Of course, through most of their history Jews did not have any choice in the matter, and all matzahs were of the hand-made variety, usually baked at home or in a communal oven. It was therefore quite a momentous turn of events when the Industrial Revolution came along and redefined a practice that had remained virtually unchanged since Moses' time.

---

* *The Jewish Free Press,* Calgary, April 4, 1998, pp. 12–13.

The turning point came in 1857 in Austria, where the first mechanical Matzah device was put to work. The machine was designed to knead the dough, squeeze it through a set of metal rollers, perforate it, and deliver the pieces promptly to be baked in the oven.

At that stage, the notion of a square matzah had not yet occurred to anyone, and this gave rise to some serious halakhic questions. The roundness of the matzahs was achieved with a sort of cookie cutter; and in the quest for efficiency, the leftover corners were then re-gathered and combined with the new dough. This raised fears lest, by allowing the dough to circulate too long between kneading and baking, it might actually start to leaven. In order to avoid such a dreadful eventuality, our beloved square matzah came into being. Continual improvements in the speed of the matzah machines increased its acceptability among many Jews.

However, not all Jewish leaders were pleased with the new developments, and several prominent rabbis voiced their opposition to the newfangled matzah machines.

The struggle against innovation was spearheaded by the celebrated Rabbi Solomon Kluger of Brody, who immediately issued a directive forbidding the use of mechanically prepared matzah on Passover.

Rabbi Kluger's objections were based on a number of considerations. Primary among them was the old fear that, even after the switch to square matzahs, bits of old dough could still adhere to the gears and cogs of the mechanism longer than the time period permitted by the halakhah. Complex machinery was, after all, difficult to keep clean.

With the advent of milling machines, which were usually steam-powered, additional fears were aroused when moisture was seen to condense in the machines due to the heat that they generated, creating lumps in the flour. That problem would later be eased somewhat by the introduction of electronic devices.

Furthermore, Rabbi Kluger noted that the time-honoured parameters established by the ancient rabbis, including the strict eighteen-minute limit for preparation of the dough, had all presupposed a manual process. Since we possess no equivalent traditions about how to deal with an automated bakery, it would be prudent to avoid any new methods.

And even if we could be convinced that the process can be engineered so as to overcome all our fears of inadvertent leavening, there remain some thorny problems that related to the religious status of matzah on Passover. After all, the matzah that is consumed at the *seder* is intended to fulfill a religious precept, and must be fashioned with the appropriate intention. We can hardly speak of a machine having any kind of intention.

Marshalling his objections and those of similarly minded scholars, Rabbi Kluger published his prohibition in 1859 in a widely distributed pamphlet bearing the title *Moda'ah le-veit yisra'el*, "a Declaration to the House of Israel." Within the year, a refutation was issued by one of the influential halakhic authorities of the day, Rabbi

Joseph Saul Nathanson of Lemberg. He titled his pamphlet "the Annulment of the Declaration."

Rabbi Nathanson argued that the rapid speed of the automated process actually made it preferable to the older methods. He was satisfied that the machinery was capable of being adequately cleaned and inspected.

There ensued a lengthy exchange of diatribes in the newspapers, in which the authors did not refrain from indulging in the most vitriolic of personal attacks.

All this squabbling seems to be utterly divorced from reality, ostensibly providing yet another instance of the rabbis' excessive concern for trivial technical details. However, careful reading of the literature reveals that there were some important economic and social issues at stake.

Nineteenth-century European society was witnessing widespread unemployment as vast numbers of agricultural and industrial workers were being replaced by efficient machines. These were the same circumstances that had incited the English Luddites to go on rampages of machine smashing. The opponents of automated matzah production feared that this same scenario would now be played out in small Jewish communities, where temporary employment at the matzah bakery frequently provided an important source of supplementary income for poor Jews who needed the money to purchase holiday provisions.

The supporters of the mechanized process were also concerned for the fate of the poor. However, they saw the matter from the opposite perspective, observing that mass production would help lower the burdensome cost of the holiday grocery basket.

But most of all, the battle over matzah machines must be viewed in the context of the deep rifts that were splitting European Judaism at the time. Experience had taught the traditionalists to be wary of *any* departure from accepted practice, even where it did not involve any overt violation of Jewish law. The dreaded Reform movement had begun by questioning minor customs and had ended up (as the traditionalists saw it) denying fundamental Jewish values!

This underlying suspicion was articulated by the rabbi of Gur in his correspondence with the rabbi of Radomsk in 1908:

> *It is clear from the actions of those who are permissive that their real desire is to remove little by little something from each mitzvah with the intention of ultimately uprooting everything.... Consequently we are obliged to stand firm in the breach, especially in this generation when, if we are lenient with regard to forbidden things, especially with regard to the prohibition of leaven on Passover, the heart of the Torah, it is against the heart of the Torah that they stretch their hands.*

Seen in this light, it is surprising how unsuccessful the traditionalists were in spreading their opposition to machine-made matzahs. By the early twentieth century, virtually all Orthodox Jewish communities had embraced the permissive position.

Halakhic integrity is unquestionably an important matter, as is ideological struggle.

But who can resist for long the allure of a new technology?

Suggestions for Further Reading

Freehof, Solomon Bennett. *The Responsa Literature and A Treasury of Responsa*. [New York]: KTAV, 1973.

Goodman, Philip. *The Passover Anthology,* 1st paperback ed. *JPS Holiday Anthologies*. Philadelphia: Jewish Publication Society of America, 1993.

Jacobs, Louis. *A Tree of Life: Diversity, Flexibility, and Creativity in Jewish Law, Littman Library of Jewish Civilization*. Oxford and New York: Oxford University Press, 1984.

Kitov, Eliyahu. *The Book of Our Heritage: the Jewish Year and Its Days of Significance*. Jerusalem: Feldheim, 1978.

Zevin, Shelomoh Yosef. *The Festivals in Halachah: An Analysis of the Development of the Festival laws,* translated by M. Holder and U. Kaploun. *ArtScroll Judaica classics*. New York and Jerusalem: Mesorah Publications and Hillel Press, 1999.

Freshly Baked: A Matzah Mystery*

It is the afternoon before Passover. The last crumbs of leavened bread were set aflame in the morning. The walls and counter-tops are scoured to a gleaming shine. The regular dishes have been hauled down to the cellar, and the special holiday utensils now sit proudly in the kitchen cupboards. Stacked in the corner are boxes of crisp matzahs ready to be consumed at the Seder.

At last it is possible to relax in anticipation of this evening's festive meal.

What is wrong with this picture?

If you were a Jew living in the early medieval era, the obvious answer would be: those boxes of prepared matzah.

According to the vast majority of authorities on Jewish law and custom at that time, it was strictly forbidden to make use of matzahs that had been baked earlier than the day preceding the seder, the fourteenth of Nissan.

---

* *Ha'Atid, the Magazine of the Melbourne Hebrew Congregation,* Summer 2002 (5:3:19), pp 11–12.

The prohibition against advance baking of matzah was expressed most uncompromisingly by the rabbis of Ashkenaz (Germany) in the tenth and eleventh centuries. For them, the ban extended even to matzah that was baked on the morning of the fourteenth of Nissan – and even if the leaven had already been completely removed from the household.

Initially, most authorities insisted that matzahs that were baked too early were completely invalid, though a few were ready to permit them after the fact.

The Ashkenazic authorities proposed several theories to explain the origins of the prohibition. Some regarded it as an instance of the talmudic principle "a mitzvah is more beloved when it is performed at its proper time" (*Pesahim* 68b, etc.). The invocation of this principle is, however, decidedly awkward, since it is usually cited in order to encourage the *early* performance of a precept, not postponing it to the last minute.

A more significant objection to this explanation lies in the fact that the "mitzvah" – the biblical commandment – of matzah is not the *baking*, but the *eating*. This is readily demonstrated by the fact that there is no blessing prescribed for baking, though there is one recited before eating the matzah at the seder: "Blessed are you ... who has ... commanded us to *eat* matzah."

Indeed, it is precisely on this point that the elders of medieval Ashkenaz appear to have had a distinctive understanding of the religious status of matzah-baking.

From the extensive discussions in the halakhic literature of the time, we learn that they did regard the baking of the matzahs as a commandment in its own right.

Only by accepting this premise can we appreciate why they frequently invoked a ruling from the Talmud that forbids the eating of matzah before noon on the eve of Passover (*Pesahim* 99b), treating it as analogous to the Passover sacrifice, which could only be offered up from the afternoon and onwards. In practical terms, this meant that the baking could not commence until about 1:30 p.m.

The celebrated French commentator Rashi treated the prohibition of earlier baking as Torah-based, and he refused to compromise even in those bothersome situations occasioned by Saturday night seders.

The solution to this mystery may lie in a better understanding of the origins of early Ashkenazic religious customs, a phenomenon that is closely linked to the question of the community's historical origins.

As has become increasingly evident to historians of rabbinic literature, the roots of many peculiar Ashkenazic customs can be traced to the Jerusalem Talmud and to other documents that preserve the religious norms of the ancient Jewish communities of the Holy Land.

This phenomenon is undoubtedly a reflection of the ethnic origins of German Jewry's founding fathers, many of whom had come to central Europe from Italy, whose Jewish community continued for many centuries to accept the authority of the Israeli leadership. Much of the analytic hairsplitting that typifies rabbinic scholarship in medieval Germany and France can be credited to their attempts to create a harmony between their own time-honoured customs and the authority of the Babylonian Talmud, which had subsequently been accepted universally by mainstream Judaism.

Now, when we examine what the Jerusalem Talmud has to say about our controversy, we soon observe that it takes a very different approach to the preparation of objects for ritual use.

Thus, in contrast to the Babylonian norm, the rabbis of the Land of Israel prescribed special benedictions to be recited over the fashioning of *tzitzit*, *t'fillin*, a *sukkah* or *lulav*, as well as other items that are used for the fulfillment of biblical precepts. The familiar Babylonian practice, on the other hand, is to recite the benedictions only when the commandment is actually being performed (e.g., by wearing the *tzitzit* or *t'fillin*, sitting in the *sukkah* or taking hold of the *lulav* during the festival; see *Menahot* 42a–42b).

It would appear that this approach to the performance of *mitzvot* provides us with the key to understanding how the early Ashkenazic rabbis were moved to equate the time limits for the Passover sacrifice with those of the baking of matzah. For them, the preparation of the matzah was as inseparable a part of the precept as the act of eating it at the seder.

From the twelfth century onwards, as the authority of the Babylonian Talmud became progressively more entrenched in the academies of France and Germany, we observe a very gradual erosion of the prohibitions against early baking of matzah.

The demographic growth of the Jewish populace also played a part in weakening the authority of the older practice. As families and communities became larger, the prospect of baking an ample stock of matzah in time for the seder became very unlikely. Of course, this difficulty became more severe in years when the baking had to be done on Saturday night, leaving insufficient time to conduct the Seder, since the *afikoman* had to be consumed before midnight, and it was important that the children remain alert for the recitation of the Haggadah.

Baking on a festival also raised some thorny halakhic questions regarding the separation of the priestly portion of the dough (*hallah*) – normally prohibited on holy days – and the cleaning and disposal of the equipment.

As a result, commentators began to speak of the last-minute baking, not as an indispensable requirement, but merely as a recommended practice; and they became more amenable to setting aside the old practice when Passover occurred directly after the Sabbath.

Some texts confined the restrictions to the three *matzot* that are obligatory at the Seder, and not (as in the earlier discussions) to *all* the matzot that are consumed during the holiday week. Eventually, some rabbis were emboldened to reject the prohibition outright, on the grounds that it was not found in the Babylonian Talmud.

The insistence on last-minute matzah-baking eventually came to be viewed as an act of extraordinary piety rather than an inflexible norm. The fifteenth-century

Bohemian authority on liturgical custom Rabbi Jacob Moelin (Maharil) summarized that the sages were split on the matter between those who preferred that the baking take place just before the seder (even on the second night!), and those who would rather have the matzahs ready in advance.

Although the permissive approach eventually prevailed among most European Jews, the ancient practice persisted tenaciously, especially in the Rhineland communities. As late as the seventeenth century, communities like Frankfurt a/M continued to bake their matzah on the fourteenth of Nissan.

The study of Jewish customs, their reasons and origins, always provides for fascinating discussion of symbolism, values, and halakhic reasoning.

But there is a unique value to studying these customs as historical artifacts. Because of their tenacious determination to continue the traditional practices of their ancestors, those early Ashkenazic Jews have succeeded in preserving valuable clues to obscure mysteries of the Jewish past.

Suggestions for Further Reading

Marcus, Ivan G. *Piety and Society: The Jewish Pietists of Medieval Germany.* Études sur le Judaisme Médiéval, edited by G. Vajda. Leiden: Brill, 1991.

Ta-Shma, Israel. "When Should Passover Matzah Be Baked?" In *Jubilee Volume in Honor of Moreinu Hagaon Rabbi Joseph B. Soloveitchik,* edited by S. Israeli, N. Lamm, and Y. Raphaei, 2, 1286–96. Jerusalem and New York: Mosad Harav Kook and Yeshiva University, 1984 [Hebrew].

———. *Early Franco-German Ritual and Custom.* Jerusalem: Magnes Press, 1992 [Hebrew].

———. *Ritual, Custom and Reality in Franco-Germany, 1000–1350.* Jerusalem: Magnes Press, 1996 [Hebrew].

Tabory, J. "'Al Afiyyat Massah Be-'Erev Pesah." *Sinai* 84 (1980): 83–85.

Zevin, Shelomoh Yosef. *The Festivals in Halachah: An Analysis of the Development of the Festival Laws.* Translated by Meir Holder and Uri Kaploun. Artscroll Judaica Classics. New York and Jerusalem: Mesorah Publications and Hillel Press, 1999.

Zimmer, Eric. *Society and Its Customs: Studies in the History and Metamorphosis of Jewish Customs,* edited by I. Gafni *et al.* Jerusalem: Merkaz Zalman Shazar Le-Toledot Yisra'el, 1996.

The 'Omer Season

The Torah (as interpreted by the rabbis) commands that a sheaf [Hebrew: *'omer*] of barley be offered following the first day of Passover, commencing a counting of seven weeks that culminates with the holiday of Shavu'ot. While the original biblical ritual is evidently an expression of thanksgiving for the grain harvest, the Jews of the Middle Ages came to observe the "*'Omer* season" as a time of quasi-mourning for various national tragedies in ancient and medieval times.

The thirty-third day of the period, known in Hebrew as Lag Ba-'omer, emerged as a festive day with distinctive themes and customs.

Counting the Days*

The Torah does not stress the connection between the beginning of the counting of the *'Omer* and the commemoration of the Exodus on Passover. Nor does it identify Shavu'ot, at the conclusion of the *'Omer* count, as the anniversary of the revelation of the Torah at Sinai. It was the Jewish oral tradition that interpreted the counting as extending from the second day of Passover until the sixth of Sivan, thereby spanning those two momentous historical milestones (see *Menahot* 65a–65b).

Nevertheless, the sages of the Talmud and Midrash interpreted the *'Omer*-related rituals in their original biblical sense as expressions of thanksgiving for the grain harvest, and as preconditions for consumption of the new barley and wheat crops (e.g., *Leviticus Rabbah* 28:2).

It was left largely to the medieval rabbis to redefine the *'Omer* count in a manner appropriate to its historical and theological associations.

---

* *The Jewish Free Press*, Calgary, April 29, 1999, p. 16.

A simple, but classic, explanation in that spirit was offered by Maimonides. In his *Guide of the Perplexed* (3:43), he wrote that the obligation to count the days from Passover to Shavu'ot teaches us that the liberation from Egyptian slavery acquires full spiritual significance only when it is perceived as the prelude to the giving of the divine law of the Torah. It follows from this that Shavu'ot is the most important of the festivals, and we therefore count the days until its arrival "just as one who is expecting his most intimate friend on a certain day counts the days, and even the hours."

The rationalist Maimonides thus remains true to form in his subordination of political liberation to the spiritual and moral enlightenment that is embodied in the Torah. His explanation seems to utterly ignore the more concrete, agricultural components of the biblical commandment, the waving of the barley sheaf at the start of the count and the offering of wheaten loaves at its conclusion, though some other interpreters noted that spiritual purification can be likened allegorically to separating grain from chaff.

Several commentators preferred to express the Israelites' feelings of anticipation through parables and symbols. The influential fourteenth-century Spanish liturgical authority Rabbi David Abudraham cited an otherwise unknown midrash that compared the Hebrews' situation to that of "a person who was incarcerated in a prison, who cried out to the king to set him free and give him his daughter in marriage. He continued to count until the awaited time." Though the situation in this parable is patently contrived, the sheer chutzpah of the prisoner's demands aptly expresses the polar contrast between the dire predicament from which the Hebrews had been rescued and the exalted state to which they were aspiring.

The mystical imagination of the medieval Kabbalistic masterpiece, the Zohar, built upon similar ideas in order to weave the theme of counting into an intricate fabric of symbols.

The Zohar alludes to another instance where the Torah speaks of an obligation to count days, namely in measuring the period of impurity before a woman is permitted to resume relations with her husband (Leviticus 15:28). This, declares the Zohar, is an appropriate metaphor for the state of the ancient Hebrews, who had been immersed for centuries in the absolute depravity of Egyptian heathenism, and were now required to undergo a process of purification in order to ready themselves for their ultimate spiritual encounter with the Almighty at Mount Sinai.

This bold erotic imagery is typical of the Kabbalistic portrayals of the divine-human encounter. The Shekhinah, God's presence among the exiled Jewish people, is often personified as a princess who has become tragically separated from her princely beloved.

Unlike Maimonides' interpretation, which has a decidedly theoretical and historical quality, whether as a declaration of religious priorities or as the reliving of a past event, the Zohar's explanation expresses a vivid immediacy. From the perspective of the Jewish mystic, we are not merely recalling an event from our collective past, but each of us is personally reliving the spiritual longing for our own Sinai experience.

The commentators we have cited do not pose the question of why, if its purpose is to express impatient anticipation, the counting does not take the form of a reverse "countdown" of the number of days remaining until Shavu'ot. Indeed, the latter possibility would seem to be precluded by the fact that the Israelites were apparently not notified in advance on which day they would be receiving the Torah.

This odd fact is consistent with the Torah's general reticence about the date and historical significance of Shavu'ot. An incisive interpretation of this puzzling phenomenon was offered by the famous Polish Jewish preacher Rabbi Solomon Ephraim Luntshitz (d. 1619) in his K'li Yekar commentary to Leviticus 23:26, in a charming explanation of why Shavu'ot, uniquely among the annual festivals, is not assigned an identifiable date on the calendar.

> *This is so because the Torah must remain as new for each person every day as it was on that day when it was received from Mount Sinai. For the Lord chose not to define a specific date, since on each and every day of the year it should appear to us as if on that day we received it from Mount Sinai....*

Suggestions for Further Reading

Leibowitz, Nehama. *Studies in Vayikra (Leviticus)*. Jerusalem: World Zionist Organization Department for Torah Education and Culture in the Diaspora, 1982.

Segal, Eliezer. "The Exegetical Craft of the Zohar: Towards an Appreciation." *AJS Review* 17(1) (1992): 31–49.

Notes from the Underground*

A tradition from the early Middle Ages links the morose character of the *'Omer* period with the talmudic passage that speaks of twelve thousand pairs of Rabbi Akiva's disciples who perished during this period (*Yevamot* 62b).

Because Rabbi Akiva was known to be a supporter of the rebel general Bar Kokhba, many modern interpreters have assumed that the events referred to are related to that historical episode, and that the students were really soldiers in the rebellion that took place in the years 132–135 C.E. that restored Jewish independence to Judea for three years, before it was savagely suppressed by the Romans. This was in spite of the fact that the Talmud ascribes their deaths to a plague, brought upon them as punishment for their lack of respect for one another.

It was not long ago that any reference to Bar Kokhba would have been looked upon with great suspicion by respectable historians. Our sources for the episode were limited to a few disconnected and cryptic passages in the Talmud, a quote from the Roman historian Dio Cassio

* *The Jewish Free Press*, Calgary, May 1, 2000, pp. 8–9.

preserved in an unreliable anthology, and an occasional coin dated "to the liberation of Israel." Yigael Yadin's dramatic excavation of Bar Kokhba's command post in the early 1960s, complete with its extensive documentary archive and other archaeological artifacts, has eliminated any remaining doubts about the historicity of the rebellion and of its powerful leader, and of its deep impact on Jewish history and society.

The spades of Israeli archaeologists have continued to unearth material that corroborates ancient reports that were only recently dismissed as legendary exaggerations.

Probably the most dramatic of these reassessments has related to Dio Cassio's account that the Jewish rebels, in their realization that they would be handicapped in any frontal confrontation with the Roman legions,

> *occupied the advantageous positions in the country and strengthened them with mines and walls, in order that they might have places of refuge whenever they should be hard pressed, and might meet together unobserved under ground; and they pierced these subterranean passages from above at intervals to let in air and light.*

This image of an intricate network of underground tunnels and bunkers, all of them meticulously prepared in the years preceding the insurrection under the very eyes of the Roman armies, was too fantastic to be given credence by respectable historians – that is, until such caves and tunnels began to be uncovered in archaeological excavations. To date, more than three hundred such complexes have been identified.

Exploiting the many natural caves that typify the topography of the region, and building upon the existing infrastructure of cisterns, wine- and oil-presses, storehouses, and burial caves, the tunnel complexes were cut into rock and linked together by horizontal and vertical passages.

The prudent planners of the network provided shafts for ventilation, tanks for water, storage rooms for food and other necessities of a long stay underground. The tunnels were situated in villages and towns scattered throughout the Judean plains, particularly along the roads, where they served strategic functions in a guerilla war. The absence of natural light made them easy to conceal from the Romans. During the early stages of the rebellion from 132 to 134, when the Romans were on the defensive, it was possible for the Jews to expand the network extensively.

In spite of the initial insistence of some skeptics that the tunnels did not necessarily date from the Bar Kokhba era, several of them contain coins and other remnants that link them precisely to those years. The numismatic evidence suggests that the Jews did not take refuge in the caves until the final year of the campaign, when the military tide had turned in favour of the Romans.

Another ancient tradition that has been re-evaluated in the light of recent archeological discoveries has to do with an obscure law in the Mishnah that forbids the wearing of "nailed sandals" on the Sabbath. The

Talmud (*Shabbat* 60a) traces the prohibition to a tragic occurrence that occurred "in the final days of the 'persecution' [*sh'mad*]," a standard rabbinic expression for the Bar Kokhba insurrection. A group of Jews who were hiding in a sealed-off cave spotted the tracks of a nailed sandal that had inadvertently been worn backwards, and assumed that enemy soldiers had entered their cave. In the ensuing panic, which took place on a Saturday, "more people were killed than were slain by the enemy."

A variant of the story had it that it was the familiar scratching sound of the sandals' nail-heads on the ground outside the cave that gave rise to the hysteria, with its deadly consequences.

Indeed, the dreaded nailed sandal was often equated in ancient sources with the might of the Roman legionary, and the word *kalgas,* from the Latin *caliga,* an army boot, became a Hebrew synonym for a fierce soldier.

Nevertheless, the talmudic rationale for the prohibition of wearing nailed sandals on the Sabbath was dismissed by most serious scholars as too farfetched for serious consideration.

Here again, archaeology has altered our perspectives on the matter.

On a mountainous ridge overlooking Jericho, a cave was excavated in 1986, and it became clear that it was one of those caves that had served as a refuge for Jews during the Bar Kokhba uprising. The cave also contained the remains of a nailed sandal that had evidently belonged to a Jewish revolutionary. The owner of the sandal evidently perished in the cave, along with more than thirty men and women of diverse ages. This tragic episode, or one very much like it, might lie at the root of the halakhic prohibition against wearing the lethal footwear.

No doubt, the soil of Israel will continue to reveal to us many more secrets that will add meaning and relevance to our religious and historical traditions.

Suggestions for Further Reading

Eshel, Hanan, and David Amit. *Refuge Caves of the Bar Kokhba Revolt.* Tel-Aviv: Eretz, The Israel Exploration Society, College of Judea and Samaria; C. G. Foundation, 1998 [Hebrew].

Isaac, Benjamin, and Aharon Oppenheimer. "The Revolt of Bar Kokhba: Ideology and Modern Scholarship." *Journal of Jewish Studies* 36(1) (1985): 33–60.

Kloner, Amos, and Yigal Tepper. *The Hiding Complexes in the Judean Shepelah.* Tel-Aviv: Hakibbutz Hameuchad Publishing House, 1987 [Hebrew].

Just a Little Bit off the Top, Please*

At the time that our first-born came into this world, the adjacent hospital bed was occupied by a mother and child from Fiji. The Fijian infant was graced with a healthy crop of black hair. A few days after the birth, we happened to meet the proud mother in the park, and a glance into the carriage revealed that her baby's beautiful hair had been shaved off. The mother explained to us that the shearing was part of a Fijian religious custom.

Contemplating our own child's shiny bald pate, we offered silent thanks that he had not been born a Fijian.

The classical Jewish sources offer some definite guidelines about *how* to cut hair, but say virtually nothing about *when* this procedure should be carried out. For example, the Torah prohibited the shaving of the sideburns (Leviticus 19:27), and the talmudic discussion concerned itself with the precise definition of what counts as a sideburn for purposes of this law (*Qiddushin* 35b). However, nowhere in the Bible or Talmud do we

* *The Jewish Free Press*, Calgary, May 3, 2000, pp. 12–13.

find any indication of a special ritual for the first cutting of the hair.

In the abundant body of medieval literature that was devoted to the meticulous description of personal and local customs, whether in Germany, France, Spain, or other centres of Jewish habitation, we hear not a single mention of any obligatory time or method for a child's first haircut.

As was true with respect to many areas in Jewish religious customs, a fundamental turning point occurred in the sixteenth century among the residents of the mystic town of Safed.

The disciples of the renowned Kabbalistic teacher Rabbi Isaac Luria (the "Ari") reported that their revered teacher used to go to the tomb of Rabbi Simeon ben Yohai in Meron to cut the hair of his young son "in accordance with the well-known custom." The day was celebrated as a virtual festival.

Evidently, Rabbi Luria's custom was not associated with a particular date on the calendar. A later tradition cited in his name associated the first haircut with the child's third birthday. Among the Safed mystics, the custom arose of cutting the haircut on Lag Ba-'omer, which was celebrated as the *yahrzeit* of Rabbi Simeon ben Yohai, who was venerated as alleged author of the Zohar, the central document of Kabbalistic teaching. Lag Ba-'omer became the occasion of a festive pilgrimage to Rabbi Simeon's tomb in Meron.

It is impossible to trace the origins of this "well-known custom," inasmuch as Safed itself had virtually no Jewish history prior to its rise to eminence in the days of Rabbi Luria and his school following the expulsion of the Jews from Spain and Portugal.

An important clue to the practice's source is suggested by the fact that it was usually referred to as *halaqah*, from an Arabic word designating the cutting of hair. Indeed, examination of Middle Eastern folk practices reveals that offerings of hair were used for diverse religious purposes, including vicarious sacrifice, fulfillment of vows (in a manner reminiscent of the biblical Nazirite; see Numbers 6:5), or as a rite of passage.

A ceremony called *'Aqiqah* is performed by many Muslims on the third, seventh, or eighth day after a birth, and it is often associated with the baby naming. The ceremony normally included a ritual cutting of the infant's first hair, alongside the offering of an animal sacrifice.

Of especial relevance to our topic is the custom among Arab mothers of consecrating their children to God or to a saint in return for a safe childbirth. At some subsequent point in the lad's life, his hair is ritually cut at a religious sanctuary or shrine as payment of the vow. Until the completion of the vow, it was forbidden to cut the child's hair. This practice is attested among the Muslims of Safed.

Among Greek Catholics in northern Syria, a collective shearing of twelve-year-old boys was held on April 23, a date that is intriguingly close to that of Lag Ba-'omer.

Early descriptions of the Jewish haircutting ritual also stipulate that the hair should be weighed, and its equivalent in silver or gold donated to religious or charitable purposes. This element is also common to most of the non-Jewish versions of the practice.

Although the ritual came to be identified with the Lag Ba-'omer festivities at Meron, the timing was subject to several variations. Many Sepharadic Jews preferred to hold it in the synagogue during the intermediate days of Passover. In Yemen, a festive cutting of the bridegroom's curls was incorporated into wedding ceremonies. On that occasion, the couple's three-year-old relatives were also given their first haircuts.

In reality, the practice of offering one's hair for a religious purpose is a very ancient one and was very widespread among the ancient Greeks. It was customary for youths in those days to shave their heads, or a particular lock that was grown for that purpose, as part of a coming-of-age rite, offering it to Apollo, Heracles, or a river god. These rituals were frequently associated with boisterous carousing and were singled out by the rabbis of the Talmud as idolatrous acts that should not be emulated or assisted by self-respecting Jews (even if they happened to be barbers).

The Kabbalistic and Hasidic circles who rediscovered these dubious customs many centuries later possessed a marvellous flare for providing ingenious prooftexts to justify them.

A favourite precedent was the biblical law of *orlah* that forbids the eating of fruit until after the tree has passed its third year (Leviticus 19:23–24). An old midrashic text had drawn a general symbolic comparison between the fruit and a human child (*Tanhuma*

Qedoshim 14), inspiring later rabbis to extend the analogy to the child's first haircut, which marks a significant milestone in the maturing process.

Even more clever was a tradition ascribed to Rabbi Isaac Luria himself, based on the Torah's procedures for purifying one afflicted with a skin disease. At a certain stage in the process, the Torah (Leviticus 13:33) requires that the patient's hair be shaved. The Hebrew word for "shave" [*vehitgalah*] is standardly written with an oversized *gimmel*, a letter that has the numerical value of three. This calligraphic peculiarity was seized upon as a biblical mandate for the practice of cutting the hair of three-year-old boys!

Whether under the Arabic name *halaqah* or its Yiddish equivalent *upsheren*, the religious ceremonies for the first haircut were generally confined to specific communities of Sepharadic Kabbalists or east European Hasidim. In recent years they have enjoyed a more general popularity, especially among the newly observant who are often thirsting for rituals and not particularly discerning about where those rituals originated.

As with many folk customs, it is difficult to draw precise lines between the diverse elements of pagan superstition, inter-religious borrowing, mystical secrets, and normative Jewish observance.

The distinctions between these realms can be as thin as a hair.

Suggestions for Further Reading

Elmslie, W. A. L. *The Mishna on Idolatry 'Aboda Zara*, edited by J. A. Robinson. Vol. 8, Texts and Studies Contributions to Biblical and Patristic Literature. Cambridge: Cambridge University Press, 1911.

Finkelman, Shimon, Nosson Scherman, Salamon Avrohom Y, and Meir Zlotowitz. *Shavuos: Its Observance, Laws, and Significance*, edited by N. Scherman and M. Zlotowitz. *ArtScroll Mesorah Series*. New York: Mesorah Publications, 1995.

Hallpike, Christopher R. "Hair." In *The Encyclopedia of Religion*, edited by M. Eliade and C. J. Adams. New York and London: Collier Macmillan, 1986.

Kafih, Joseph. *Jewish Life in Sanà, Studies and Texts: Publications of the Ben-Zvi Institute*. Jerusalem: Ben-Zvi Institute of the Hebrew University, 1982.

Krauss, S. *Qadmoniyyot ha-Talmud*. Berlin, Vienna, Tel-Aviv, 1924–45.

Lieberman, Saul. *Tosefta ki-fshutah*. New York: The Jewish Theological Seminary of America, 1973.

Morgenstern, Julian. *Rites of Birth, Marriage, Death and Kindred Occasions among the Semites*. New York: Ktav, 1974.

Nicolson, Frank W. "Greek and Roman Barbers," *Harvard Studies in Classical Philology* 2 (1891): 41–56.

Sperber, Daniel. *Minhage Yisra'el: Meqorot Ve-Toladot*, Jerusalem: Mosad ha-Rav Kuk, 1989.

Zevin, Shelomoh Yosef. *The Festivals in Halachah: An Analysis of the Development of the Festival laws*, translated by M. a. K. Holder, Uri. *ArtScroll Judaica classics*. New York and Jerusalem: Mesorah Publications and Hillel Press, 1999.

The Case of the Missing 'Omer*

In the days when the Jerusalem Temple stood at the centre of Jewish religious observance, the offering of the *'omer* of barley on the second day of Passover was one of the most beloved of sacred rites. Not until that first sheaf of grain was harvested and offered as a sacrifice was it permissible to partake of the new grain crop (Leviticus 23:9–14).

The Mishnah stipulates that it is preferable to bring the *'omer* of barley from the vicinity of Jerusalem, as an expression of our zeal to perform the precept as quickly as possible. However, if the grain there has not yet ripened sufficiently, it may be brought from elsewhere (*Menahot* 10:2). As an illustration of such a case, the Mishnah mentions an occasion when the *'omer* was brought from "*Gagot Serifin.*" Scholars have identified this name with the town of Sarafand near Lydda.

Though the context of the Mishnah seems to suggest that the need to fetch barley from outside Jerusalem was the result of natural delays in crop growth, rabbinic

* *The Jewish Free Press*, Calgary, May 2, 2002, pp. 8, 10.

tradition speaks of a more ominous background to the episode. According to the Talmud, the dearth of suitable grain in the Jerusalem area was the result of a civil war that was being waged by two rival claimants to the Hasmonean throne, Hyrcanus and Aristobulus (*Menahot* 64b). This incident, which took place in 66 B.C.E., is also described by Josephus Flavius. As Hyrcanus's forces were laying siege to the holy city, Aristobulus's followers were confined within the walls. It was under these conditions that the need arose to seek out barley from other regions.

The talmudic account goes on to describe the peculiar manner in which the barley was procured. Initially, the community was at a loss to locate an alternate source, so they issued a call to anyone who could point them to a place from which to harvest the precious sheaves. In the end, the only person who responded to the call was a deaf-mute who bewildered everybody with incomprehensible charades. He positioned one hand on a roof and the other on a shed. Eventually, the signal was deciphered by one of the Temple officials, a certain Petahiah who was renowned for his astounding linguistic abilities. Petahiah concluded that "roofs" in Hebrew are *gagot* and sheds are *serifin*. Once it was established that there was a locality named *Gagot Serifin*, the necessary barley for the *'omer* ritual was acquired from there.

Traditional commentators had difficulties accounting for some of the details in this story. For one thing, it stretches our credulity to suggest that the effects of the siege were so extreme that not even a modest measure of barley could be procured in the Jerusalem area. It is equally puzzling that nobody but the deaf-mute knew the whereabouts of the barley, and that the message could not be conveyed in a more direct manner.

Basing himself on anomalies of this sort, Rabbi Solomon Eidels (the Maharsha) arrived at the conclusion that the shortage of barley was not an indirect or collateral result of the siege, but must have been part of a deliberate policy to suppress the performance of the precept. This premise makes it easier to understand why the entire barley supply had been systematically destroyed. It also helps explain why the whereabouts of the barley at *Gagot Serifin* were kept secret and divulged only to a deaf-mute, so that it would have to be decoded like a carefully protected password. In this way, the information was less likely to fall into the hands of hostile parties. Rabbi Jacob Ibn Habib saw in the choice of the deaf-mute a symbolic disparagement of a contentious generation who metaphorically "closed their ears" to words of Torah.

In fact, Josephus provides some interesting historical details that help elucidate why there was no barley available for the *'omer* ritual.

Josephus, in agreement with talmudic traditions, describes an accord that called for the priests inside Jerusalem to lower a sum of money over the city walls in a basket, in return for which the besieging forces would send up sheep for the daily sacrifices. On one occasion, Hyrcanus violated the agreement by sending up pigs instead of sheep. So indignant were the priests at this blasphemous provocation that they beseeched God to exact vengeance on the perpetrators. In what was interpreted by contemporaries as an act of supernatural retribution, there arose a fierce windstorm that utterly destroyed all the produce of the land.

Josephus' story offers us an appropriate explanation for the disappearance of barley at that point in time.

The moral issues of the story were expressed forcefully by the pious miracle-worker Onias, in an incident related by Josephus. This Onias was the same figure who appears in talmudic legend as "Honi ha-Me'aggel," famous for his unfailing ability to produce rain through his prayers (*Ta'anit* 3:8). According to Josephus, Hyrcanus tried to recruit Honi to curse Aristobulus and his faction, but the saint refused adamantly to misuse his spiritual gift to exacerbate a conflict between fellow Jews. Eventually, in spite of his repeated refusals and excuses, Honi was located and compelled to speak. At this point, he stood up and entreated the Almighty not to hearken to the prayers of either side. The outcome of Honi's noble stand was that he was stoned to death by the incensed rabble.

The combined testimony of the Talmud and Josephus Flavius can serve as a valuable lesson in the proper and improper uses of Jewish religious practice: Rituals like the *'omer* offering were intended to promote unity and concord, not to be exploited in the interests of discord and factionalism.

Israeli Independence Day

The re-emergence of Jewish statehood, with the Declaration of Independence of the State of Israel on the fifth of Iyyar 5708 (May 14, 1948), is commemorated annually on its anniversary (according to the Hebrew date) by many Jews, whether as a secular, civil, or religious festival

Gathering the Dispersed of Israel*

More than any other contemporary country, the State of Israel has been a nation of immigrants. The very first law enacted by its fledgling parliament was the Law of Return that guaranteed Israeli citizenship to any Jew who sought it. Although we are accustomed to measuring periods of Israeli history in terms of wars, it would provide a more revealing evaluation of the national spirit if we were to enumerate instead the many waves of Jewish immigration that have left their imprint on the country's cultural diversity.

At the beginnings of the Zionist movement and in the early years of the State of Israel, the chief objective of Jewish nationalists was to provide a sanctuary for the persecuted Jews of the diaspora. In contrast to the security and comfort enjoyed by Western Jewish communities, then as now, there have not been many occasions when Jews would choose to settle in the promised land for the sake of ease or tranquility. On the contrary, those who took upon themselves the commitment to "go up" to

* *The Jewish Free Press*, Calgary, May 7, 1998, pp. 10–11.

the holy land were aware that they were also being called upon to accept a lowering of their material standards of living in order to fulfill ideological and religious goals. In spite of this, there have always been Jews who were prepared to accept those hardships for the sake of the privilege of dwelling upon their ancestral soil.

We might expect that the spirit of dedication and sacrifice demonstrated by those new immigrants would be appreciated by the beleaguered populace of Israel.

However, appreciation is not always forthcoming. The Jews of the Holy Land have not always been overwhelmed with admiration for their cousins who had chosen to join them from more affluent communities abroad. There have been several examples of frictions and prejudices between the assorted ethnic groups that compose the Israeli Jewish community. One can cite many examples of intolerance directed against new immigrants.

Jews hailing from Iraq were stereotyped for the coarseness of their manners, while those from Egypt were mocked for their pride and arrogance. And there was the lamentable case of those hapless Turkish Jews who settled in a Galilean town, who were moved to lament to their rabbi about their social isolation: Nobody would even favour them with a simple "hello."

To be fair, immigrants from these distinguished diaspora communities were slow to assimilate into the local culture. They maintained their own synagogues, customs, and *Landsmanschaften* long after settling in the homeland. One nationalistic Israeli rabbi lost his composure when he encountered a clique of immigrant Jews congregating together in the street. He began chasing them away, while castigating them viciously for the failure of their families and former countrymen to immigrate to Israel *en masse*, rather than in a slow trickle! To hear the rabbi rant, these newcomers were to blame for all of Israel's troubles!

Sometimes the treatment of the immigrants has degenerated into cruelty, as in that unpleasant reception that awaited one Iraqi rabbi shortly after his arrival in the promised land. When the rabbi, a frail and diminutive individual, entered a local butcher shop in search of a cut of meat, the proprietor seems to have taken offence at the idea of this little foreigner's self-importance, and decided to play a mean trick on the arrogant greenhorn whose strange accent and outlandish dress betrayed his foreign origins.

When the rabbi inquired about the price of his purchase, he was told that it would come to "fifty shekels and a smack." In vain, the rabbi ventured an offer to raise the cash price in hope that the butcher would relinquish the smack, but ended up with a bill for "a hundred shekels and the smack." The bewildered sage was forced to submit to the humiliation, and left the shop muttering about the peculiar customs of the new land.

Before we go too far with this scathing indictment of Israeli xenophobia, one small detail should be made clear: *All of the stories related in the preceding paragraphs were quoted from the pages of the Talmud and Midrash*, and occurred more than fifteen hundred years ago. The names of the lands of immigration were modernized, of course, so that "Babylonia" became "Iraq" and "Cappadocia" became "Turkey," but the stories themselves were otherwise unchanged. [See Jerusalem Talmud *'Eruvin* 3:1 (20d); Jerusalem Talmud *Shevi'it* 9:5 (39a); *Yoma* 66b; 9b; *Song of Songs Rabbah* 8:9; Jerusalem Talmud *Berakhot* 2:8 (5c)].

Modern Israel has been characterized as a society that "loves immigration, but hates immigrants." From the perspective of history we can see that the same fundamental human attitudes have remained constant over the generations. Similar anecdotes could of course be told about the experiences of newcomers to Calgary, Toronto, or Los Angeles.

And yet, strengthened by their dedication, persistence, and resilience, as well as by the fundamental decency of the veteran citizens, most of those immigrants have ultimately succeeded in being absorbed into their intimidating new surroundings.

Of all the manifold accomplishments in which Israel can take pride, this surely ranks among the most miraculous.

Suggestions for Further Reading

Lieberman, Saul. "'Thus it was and thus it shall be' – Palestinian Jews and World Jewry during the Era of the Mishnah and the Talmud," *Cathedra* 17 (1981): 3–10 [Hebrew].

That Old Blue Box*

No symbol of commitment to the Zionist cause is more recognizable than that simple blue JNF blue box that has graced many a mantelpiece or kitchen counter over the last century.

Initially, several alternative methods were considered for collecting the donations that would be used by the Jewish National Fund to purchase lands on behalf of the Jewish people. An article that appeared in 1900 in the Zionist newspaper *Die Welt* favoured the distribution of stamp sets that could be assembled into special albums. At the same time, a "Golden Book" was established to be inscribed with the names of all patrons who had contributed at least ten pounds to the cause. While both these modern-looking ideas were implemented immediately, and with some measure of success, it took a few years before the Zionist movement hit upon their most popular fundraiser, the placing of tin collection boxes in private homes.

---

* *The Jewish Free Press*, Calgary, April 18, 2002, pp. 8–9.

This last-mentioned idea was the invention of a Galician Zionist named Haim Kleinman, who tested the method in his own locality before it earned recognition from the official bodies. Kleinman commenced by placing a single box in his office. When he reported the success of his efforts in a letter to *Die Welt* in 1902, the method was spontaneously emulated by many individuals, still without official sanction from the Zionist leadership. It was not until 1905 that the official reports included any acknowledgment of the blue boxes. Within a few decades it had become clear that the revenues collected through the blue boxes were greater by far than those brought in from any other source.

At the time of its reluctant adoption by the Zionist movement, the domestic charity box was by no means unknown to the world of Jewish philanthropy. *Pushkahs* had been in use for close to a century as a means of collecting funds for various religious causes, especially for the support of the poor in the Holy Land. Precisely these associations with the religious – and anti-Zionist – institutions of the "Old Yishuv" made many Zionists reluctant to adopt this method for their own fundraising.

The institution of the home-based charity box appears to be rooted in the waves of immigration from eastern Europe to the Holy Land that took place at the end of the eighteenth and the beginning of nineteenth centuries. This phenomenon embraced both Hasidic and anti-Hasidic (Mitnagdic) circles, the latter represented by leading disciples of the Ga'on of Vilna. Through their modest contributions to the *pushkahs*, Eastern European

Jews strengthened their identification with their brethren in Palestine. For their own part, the new immigrants did not integrate well with the veteran Jewish populace, and required a constant flow of donations in order to maintain themselves and their separate institutions. Working for one's livelihood was still not an option that was taken seriously in such intensely spiritual circles.

In contrast to the earlier situation, when the Jews of Eretz Israel were perceived as a tiny body of far-off zealots, the current crop of immigrants included many respected scholars who maintained strong links with local rabbis, communities, and relatives. Thus, it was both necessary and possible to create a solid infrastructure for the continual collection of donations from their home communities.

Although they attracted only tiny contributions and were virtually impossible to regulate in a systematic manner, the home-based coin boxes had the advantage of involving all segments of society, including women and others who did not have frequent access to charity boxes that were housed in the synagogues or other public institutions.

By 1829, a Galician *Maskil* penned a letter to the Austro-Hungarian government in which he condemned the prevalence of charity boxes as an unpatriotic subterfuge for illicitly channelling funds out of the homeland.

At the same time, the same Lithuanian scholarly circles that had played a prominent role in emigration to Palestine were also pioneering the establishment of their new model of international yeshivahs. It did not take long for them to latch on to the same successful fundraising scheme, and it became a common sight for Jewish homes to house, side by side, two different *pushkahs*: one for upkeep of the Jews of Jerusalem, and one for the Volozhin Yeshivah.

When the Jewish National Fund reluctantly decided to emulate this traditional form of alms-giving, one can easily imagine their leaders' discomfort at imitating a programme that had originated in circles whose ideology and objectives were so diametrically opposite to their own. Zionism was, after all, striving for the creation of a new secular Jewish culture in which proud workers would cultivate their own land. For the Zionists, the traditional *pushkah* denoted a society of superstitious parasites, locked into the Middle Ages, passively waiting for the redemption while living off the generosity of others.

Ironically, the JNF donation box would inherit many of the religious associations of its predecessors. Like the boxes that were intended for the collection of pennies for the poor of Jerusalem, the blue boxes would routinely be positioned next to the Shabbat candlesticks, so that the act of dropping in a coin became for many a ritual associated with the Sabbath preparations.

These kinds of paradoxical encounters between the old and the new, the traditional and the revolutionary, the extremes of militant religion and secularism, are of course an inescapable part of the Zionist experience that never fails to add to the fascination and exasperation that characterize Israeli culture.

Suggestions for Further Reading

Hirschmann, Ira. *The Awakening: The Story of the Jewish National Fund.* New York: Shengold, 1981.

Lehn, Walter, and Uri Davis. *The Jewish National Fund.* London: Kegan Paul, 1988.

Shilony, Zvi. *Ideology and Settlement: The Jewish National Fun, 1897–1914.* Translated by Fern Seckbach, Israel Studies in Historical Geography. Jerusalem: Magnes Press, 1998.

Shva, Shlomo. *One Day and 90 Years: The Story of the Jewish National Fund.* Jerusalem: Department of Publications and Audio-Visual Aids Information Division, Jewish National Fund, 1991.

Stampfer, Shaul. "The 'Collection Box': The Social Role of Eretz Israel Charity Funds." *Cathedra* 21 (1981): 89–102.

Shavu'ot

The festival of Shavu'ot [Weeks] occurs fifty days after the beginning of Passover, in late Spring. The biblical holiday celebrates the ripening of the wheat and the first summer fruits. According to the calculations of the rabbis, Shavu'ot is celebrated as the anniversary of the revelation of the Torah at Mount Sinai, the defining event of Israelite religious history.

Honey from the Tablets*

An invaluable source of information about Jewish life in earlier generations is the illuminated Hebrew manuscript. Even when illustrating Bibles or other ancient works, the artists used as their models the contemporary norms of dress, customs, and architecture, and thereby provided modern readers with unique visual glimpses into the daily life of the Middle Ages. This applies all the more when the text of the manuscript is a prayer book, describing the order of worship through the course of the Jewish calendar. For such a purpose, the illustrator is likely to base his pictures on the practices that he sees in his own community.

The above observations hold true for an elaborately illuminated prayer book from the fourteenth century that is presently housed in Leipzig. When we turn to the pages devoted to the Shavu'ot services, we should not be surprised to see a depiction of Moses clutching the tablets of the Torah on Mount Sinai. However, we might be taken aback by several representations, right next to

* *The Jewish Free Press*, Calgary, May 25, 2000, pp. 8–9.

the familiar biblical scene, of children with some strange props.

Each of the tots is proudly clutching a round cake and an egg. One of them is being carried by a beardless adult, evidently his young father, who has him wrapped in a cloak. Another child is sitting on the lap of a stern-faced rabbi who bears an uncanny resemblance to the Moses of the adjacent picture. The rabbi is clutching a writing tablet painted in the same gold leaf that was used in the artist's depiction of Moses' tablets. Two other children are being conducted to an outing by a river.

What do these images have to do with Shavu'ot?

As the anniversary of Israel's receiving the Torah, Shavu'ot was considered an appropriate time to introduce schoolchildren to their first formal religious studies. The ceremonies that evolved around that occasion take remarkably similar forms whether we are speaking of Jewish communities in France, Germany, Poland, or North Africa.

The earliest descriptions that we possess of such a celebration are from Germany in the twelfth and thirteenth centuries. One of these accounts appears in the important compendium of customs by Rabbi Eleazar Rokeah. Several other documents from the time present similar pictures.

The ceremony commences with the father, or a distinguished scholar, bringing the child to the synagogue or schoolhouse, bathed and garbed in clean attire. Upon his arrival, the rabbi carries the child to his seat. The letters of the Hebrew alphabet, or portions of it, are written frontward and backward on a writing tablet, as are some appropriate verses, such as "Moses commanded us the Torah, even the inheritance of the congregation of Jacob" (Deuteronomy 33:4).

After his first lesson in reading, the child is invited to lick some honey from the tablet. He is given a piece of honey cake on which is inscribed an appropriate biblical verse; then a boiled egg (most authors insist on three eggs) with a different text written on it. The child recites each text after the rabbi, and then is allowed to eat the cake and the egg, which are considered effective for "opening the heart."

The concern for "opening" or "broadening" the heart is emphasized in many of the texts. The allusion is to improving the memory, which was so vital to the traditional elementary curriculum. One of the texts contains an incantation to be recited against "Potah the Prince of Forgetfulness," the supernatural agent who – unless duly controlled – has the power to impair our powers of memorization. This is one of the reasons why, according to some of the accounts, the child is led afterwards to a riverbank. In addition to the well-known identification of the Torah with life-giving water, a visit to the river was believed to assist in "broadening the heart" of the fresh young student.

In keeping with the ancient tradition, the child commences his biblical studies with the Book of Leviticus, which is filled with the spirit of purity. One writer even insists that now is the perfect time to teach the child the art of swaying during his studies. The sources emphasize that in this, his first encounter with the regimen of Torah study, the child is reliving the experience of our ancestors on that very first Shavu'ot at Mount Sinai.

This special Shavu'ot celebration is outlined in very similar terms by other Jewish writers from medieval Germany. The main differences between their accounts relate to the choice of verses to be written, recited, and eaten. Some of the texts contain detailed recipes for the cakes and attach symbolic meanings to the ingredients.

Not all the foods have symbolic meanings. The sources encourage giving the children a wide assortment of treats, including nuts, apples, and other fruits, in order to implant pleasant associations with the experience of going to school. As the *Mahzor Vitry*, an important French liturgical compendium from the early twelfth century, puts it so piquantly, "first entice him, and afterwards let him feel the strap on his back."

Individual features of this celebration have been maintained informally as part of the standard way of introducing a child to his first day of school. However, in spite of the precise instructions that appear in so many compendia of Ashkenazic religious practice, no Jewish community has retained the full ritual as part of its Shavu'ot observance.

This puzzling development was noted by several rabbis in later generations, and they tried to suggest explanations for the abandonment of the ceremony. At any rate, I believe that we have good reason to sympathize with the lament of Rabbi Jacob Emden of Altona, who was mystified and dismayed at how such an admirable custom could have been uprooted from Jewish tradition for no apparent reason. He regarded this development as symptomatic of our insufficient esteem for Jewish learning.

Perhaps the time has come to take up Rabbi Emden's challenge, and to reclaim Shavu'ot's standing as a time of rededication to meaningful Jewish education.

Suggestions for Further Reading

Abrahams, Israel. *Jewish Life in the Middle Ages*. New York: Atheneum, 1969.

Asaf, S. *Meqorot le-Toledot ha-Hinnukh be-Yisra'el*. Tel-Aviv: Dvir, 1954.

Cohen, E. M. "The Teacher, the Father and the Virgin Mary in the Leipzig Mahzor." Paper read at Tenth World Congress of Jewish Studies, Jerusalem, 1990.

Marcus, Ivan G. *Rituals of Childhood: Jewish Acculturation in Medieval Europe*. New Haven: Yale University Press, 1996.

Crowning Achievement*

In retelling the events of the first Shavu'ot, about how Moses stood alone before the Almighty on Mount Sinai, the Talmud introduces some astonishing new details to the story (*Menahot* 29b).

As the rabbis tell the tale, Moses was so overcome by impatience that he could not restrain himself from complaining that the Lord was spending precious moments on what appeared to be decorative ornaments to the Hebrew letters of the Torah. To this the Creator replied that, while these ornaments might now appear superfluous, in a future generation there would arise a great scholar named Rabbi Akiva who would be able to derive heaps and heaps of new laws and teachings from those trivial-looking decorative flourishes, which are designated by the Hebrew word *tag* [plural: *tagin*].

What, indeed, were those *tagin* that were important enough to delay God's giving of the Torah?

At first glance, the answer seems a simple one, well known to anyone with a cursory knowledge of how Torah

* *Ha-Atid: Magazine of the Melbourne Hebrew Congregation*, Melbourne Australia, June–September 2000, 4:3 (15):11–12.

scrolls are written. According to the traditional practice set down in the Talmud, there are seven letters – identified by the acronym *sha'atnez getz* – that are decorated, whenever they appear in the Torah, by means of special embellishments attached to the top of the letters.

If these ornaments were the *tagin* that Moses beheld on Mount Sinai, calligraphic features that are mechanically added to the form of the letters, then it is difficult to imagine how Rabbi Akiva could have ascribed exegetical importance to them.

And in truth, when we examine the traditional commentators to the talmudic passage, we see that they understood the matter quite differently.

Rashi calls our attention to a passage that is found elsewhere in the Talmud, a delightful anecdote about how a class of schoolchildren produced a sequence of ingenious new interpretations for the names and shapes of the letters of the Hebrew alphabet (*Shabbat* 104a). According to these young prodigies, the letter *kof* stands for the word *kadosh*, and refers to the Holy One, whereas the *resh* represents *rasha*, the wicked. Accordingly, they ask, "Why is the *kof* turned away from the *resh*? It is as if the Holy One is saying: I am unable to gaze upon the wicked."

Rashi explains that that the children were basing their interpretation on the fact that the *kof* sometimes has a little *tag* ornament on its roof, like a miniature *zayin*, that faces away from the *resh* when the alphabet is written in proper sequence. As we read Rashi's comments, we sense that something is not quite right. After all, *kof* is not one of the seven letters included in the *sha'atnez getz* group, so why should it have a *tag* on its top?

Furthermore, as we study other medieval compendia of Jewish law, it quickly becomes apparent that the conventions for writing *tagin* in Torah scrolls are much more complicated than we first supposed.

One of the most important sources for the development of synagogue practice in medieval Europe is a work known as the *Mahzor Vitry*, a compendium of laws and customs that was composed by Rashi's students in twelfth-century France. From various directives contained in the *Mahzor Vitry* we learn that the *sha'atnez getz* rule was not meant to apply to every occurrence of those seven letters in the Bible, but rather to specific texts that are inscribed in a *mezuzah*. This approach finds independent corroboration in Maimonides' *Mishneh Torah*, where he deals with the *sha'atnez getz* letters only in connection with the writing of the *Shema'* in *t'fillin* and *mezuzot*. After specifying their locations and shapes, he comments: "If one neglected to include the *tagin* or wrote more or less than the required ones, this does not disqualify it."

Furthermore, we learn from the *Mahzor Vitry* that the *tagin* were not written in the way they are written today, by adding the same *zayin*-like appendage to the tops of the respective letters. Rather, there were special rules for how the letter was to be shaped each and every time it appeared.

> *The shin has five tagin: two on the first leg and two on the last, and one on the middle one. The 'ayin has three on each leg. The tet has two on the first leg and three on the last. The nun and the zayin have three apiece. The gimel has three tagin. The tzadik has two on the first leg and three on the last.*

In an addendum to this section, the editor of the *Mahzor Vitry* notes that he has witnessed the practice of decorating all the *sha'atnez getz* letters in a uniform manner, though such was not the dominant custom in his own community. Some authorities (including Rashi's grandson, Rabbi Jacob Tam), preferred to play it safe by following both practices: the individual rules should be followed with regards to the special shapes of specific letters, but in other cases the *sha'atnez getz* letters should always be decorated with their uniform *tagin*.

The *Mahzor Vitry* actually incorporates a separate treatise devoted to the minutiae of writing *tagin* in sacred texts, a work that bears the title, appropriately enough, *The Book of Tagin*. Its opening lines bear witness to the author's belief that he was in possession of a most ancient and arcane tradition that was carefully passed from teacher to disciple from the earliest times:

> *And this is the book of Tagin that Ely the Priest took up from the twelve stones that Joshua set up at Gilgal; and he handed them to Samuel, and Samuel handed them to Palti ben Laish, and Palti ben Laish handed them to Ahitofel, and Ahitofel to Ahijah the*

> *Shilonite, and Ahijah to Elijah and Elijah to Elisha and Elisha to Jehoiadah the Priest. And Jehoiadah to the prophets. And they buried it under the doorstep of the Temple. And when the doorstep of the Temple was uprooted during the reign of Jehoiachin King of Judah, Ezekiel found it and brought it to Babylonia. And during the reign of Cyrus King of Persia.... Ezra discovered this book and brought it up to Jerusalem, and it reached Menahem, and Menahem handed it over to Rabbi Nehuniah ben Hakkaneh ...*

Rabbi Moses Nahmanides accepted this claim at face value, and held the *Book of Tagin* in profound reverence, since he associated the *tagin* with the mysterious gates of understanding that had been bestowed upon Moses when God wrote out the Torah for him at Sinai. The significance of the special letters was a mysterious secret, "for these secret allusions can be known only through the oral tradition that originated with Moses at Sinai."

The traditions surrounding the *tagin* were especially important to the Jewish pietist movement known as *Hasidut Ashkenaz* that flourished in Germany in the twelfth and thirteenth centuries. The followers of this movement placed great emphasis on the mystical significance of words, and they meticulously reckoned the numerological values of each word in the prayer book. Evidently, the movement's founder Rabbi Judah the Pious composed a treatise entitled the *Book of Wisdom* in which he expounded the mysteries of the *tagin*. The colophon to that book aptly reflects the reverence in which the *tagin* were held by those circles:

> *It is forbidden to add to [the authorized list of tagin], nor may one omit even a single tag, since they are precisely as they were given at Mount Sinai. They have been passed down as an oral tradition by Elijah the Prophet to Ezra the High Priest. And the person who is punctilious about them will be blessed in this world and in the next. One must take great care not to diminish or to add even as much as a hair's breadth, for several explanations and several mysteries can be derived from them, because each one contains several interpretations. Any Torah scroll that lacks them is not fit to be read from. Therefore, all God-fearing individuals should be scrupulous with regard to them, and their reward will be great from the God of Israel....*

Maimonides also emphasized, in his rules for writing Torah scrolls, that the *tagin* should be written in their traditional manner:

> *One ought to take great care with regards to the letters that are to be written larger and the ones that are written smaller, and the ones that have dots and the ones that have unusual shapes, like the wrapped peh's and the twisted letters, as the scribes have copied one from another. And one ought to take great care with regard to the tagin and their proper number;*

> *sometimes a letter requires one tag, and there are shins that have seven of them. So too, regarding the tagin that have the shape of zayins, which are as thin as a hair.*

It is evident that Maimonides' contemporaries were mystified by the *tagin*, and he was questioned about their shapes and about whether they should be treated as an optional custom or as an indispensable requisite for kosher Torah scrolls or *mezuzahs*. After providing a brief description of some of their forms, Maimonides stated that their purpose is no longer known, nor is it possible to deduce it; though we can learn from the talmudic account of Moses' sojourn on Mount Sinai that the *tagin* had been part of Moses' original Torah scroll. Nevertheless, their omission does not disqualify the scroll, and conflicting traditions have evolved concerning their precise forms and placement.

> *Seeing as there is much disagreement on this, and since according to the strict law their omission is not grounds for disqualification, because their inclusion is only intended to imitate the scrolls that were written by our Master Moses, therefore the people of some countries preferred to omit them and to leave them out of the scrolls altogether, on account of the disagreements that surround them; for writing them would not be a faithful imitation of the above-mentioned scroll.*

Maimonides himself was of the opinion that, notwithstanding the divergence of opinions, a normative practice could be formulated based on majority usage, and that it would be preferable, though not compulsory, to follow that practice.

An attitude closer to our current practice was espoused by Rav Hai Ga'on, who headed the Babylonian academy of Pumbedita during the eleventh century. He was asked whether every occurrence of the letter *zayin* (one of the *sha'atnez getz* letters) in a *mezuzah* or *t'fillin* required a *tag*. His questioners noted that they possessed old *mezuzahs* in which only some of the letters had the *tagin*. The *Ga'on* nevertheless ruled that they were not fit unless every single *zayin* was decorated by a *tag*.

Hebrew letters with *tagin* from the Mahzor Vitry

Examination of actual Torah scrolls reveals considerable variation in the degree to which different Jewish communities tried to implement the traditions about the "strange letters." Diverse traditions of writing the "wrapped *peh*" (variants of that Hebrew letter that had extra curls inside them) were maintained quite faithfully in Yemen, Bohemia, and Germany, though we do not encounter them in texts from the Cairo Genizah.

I suppose that it should not surprise us too much that the secrets of the *tagin* have been lost over time. After all, Moses himself was unable to comprehend them! Nevertheless, it is tempting to speculate how much we would be enriched – whether in the form of Rabbi Akiva's "heaps and heaps" of laws, or Rabbi Judah the Pious' mystical insights – if only we were able to reclaim that ancient tradition.

Suggestions for Further Reading

Gaster, Moses. *The Tittle Bible: A Model Codex of the Pentateuch*. London: Maggs Bros., 1929.

Lehmann, Menashe Manfred. "'Al Pe-in Lefufin." *Bet Mikra* 30 (4) (1985): 449–55.

Razhabi, Yitzhak. "Irregular Letters in the Torah." In *Torah Shelemah*, edited by M. M. Kasher. Jerusalem: American Biblical Encyclopedia Society, 1978 [Hebrew].

Ta-Shma, I. M. "The Attitude to Aliya to Eretz Israel (Palestine) in Medieval German Jewry." *Shalem: Studies in the History of the Jews in Eretz Israel* 6 (1992): 315–18 [Hebrew].

———. "'Al Tagin ve-Ziyyunin Shel Sefer Torah." In *From the Collection of the Institute of Microfilmed Hebrew Manuscripts*, edited by A. David. Jerusalem: The Jewish National and University Library, 1996 [Hebrew].

When Mount Sinai Was Lifted Up*

Traditional Judaism has always asserted that the Torah can be understood in an infinite number of ways, as it addresses itself to the individual abilities and concerns of every person in every age and locality. This principle has also been applied to the account of the giving of the Torah itself, which we commemorate on the festival of Shavu'ot. The events at Mount Sinai have been interpreted by Jews over the ages in a rich variety of manners, reflecting the concerns and approaches of the respective commentators and their reactions to developments in the world around them.

By way of illustration, I would like to focus on one particular passage in the Sinai narrative that has lent itself to diverse interpretations. In describing the preparations for the revelation, the Torah states that "Moses brought forth the people out of the camp to meet God; and they stood beneath the mountain (Exodus 19:17)." The Hebrew phrase used here (*be-tahtit ha-har*) evidently means that they encamped at the foot of the mountain.

---

* *Chicago Jewish Star* Magazine May 25–June 7, 2001, p. 9.

However, looked at with a more narrow literalism, it can be understood as "they stood underneath the mountain"

A similar wording is employed in Deuteronomy 4:11: "And you came near and stood under the mountain [tahat ha-har]." The wording inspired commentary by a number of Jewish sages.

The renowned Rabbi Akiva, who dominated Jewish life at the beginning of the second century C.E., had a singular mystical approach to religious life. Central to his outlook was the Song of Songs, a unique biblical book which consists of sensuous love poetry. It was through Rabbi Akiva's advocacy that the Song of Songs was ultimately accepted, with opposition, into the Hebrew Bible (*Yadayim* 3:5). He believed that the eroticism of the Song was a symbolic expression of the highest degrees of individual and national intimacy with the Divine. He was guided by the powerful love imagery in some of the decisive moments of his life, including his own mystical experiences and his ultimate act of martyrdom at the hands of the Romans, a fate to which he was condemned because of his own passionate commitment to Torah. He perceived martyrdom as the ultimate expression of his love for God. It was in keeping with such a religious outlook that Rabbi Akiva regarded the revelation of the Torah at Mount Sinai as precisely the kind of immediate religious ecstasy that was being poetically portrayed in the Song of Songs.

In this spirit, some sages of the Midrash applied to the Sinai events the passionate words of the Song: "O my dove, who are in the clefts of the rock, in the crannies of the cliff (2:14)." This was expounded as if to say that God had lovingly lifted the mountain in order to offer a protective shield for his people. When the people encamped "beneath the mountain," they were doing so in the most literal manner, and God was extending over them his caring protection.

A later rabbi adapted the same image to make a totally different point, as recorded in the following well-known passage from the Babylonian Talmud:

> *"And they stood in the bottom of the mountain" – This teaches that God overturned the mountain on them like a tub and said to them: "If you accept the Torah, fine. But if you don't, then here shall be your burial!" (Shabbat 88a).*

The implications of this passage were troubling to the other talmudic sages. One rabbi argued that this would undermine the entire basis for adherence to the Torah, since according to Jewish law a commitment made under threat or duress is not considered binding. It could also be used by gentiles to deflate the pride that Jews have always taken in their willingness to obey the word of God.

Interestingly, the noted Babylonian Sage Rava resolved the problem by asserting that the real acceptance of the Torah took place in the time of Mordecai and Esther, when "the Jews ordained and took upon them and upon their seed" (Esther 9:27). Rava seems to be saying that we should be suspicious of commitments made in the heat of ardour, to the accompaniment of thunder, lightning, and assorted pyrotechnics.

What is more important and lasting is the deliberately considered decision made at a time when God's glory is not so visible, as was the case in the time of the Purim story.

A number of commentators were troubled by the fact that the above portrayal of the Israelites' acceptance of the Torah under threat runs counter to the prevalent view that they had accepted the Torah with full willingness. First, before even hearing what was contained in the Torah, they had declared unconditionally, "We shall do it!"; and only afterwards "and we shall hear" the details of its contents (Exodus 24:17).

According to one medieval view, the about-face can be resolved by distinguishing between two different Torahs. Jewish tradition recognizes that, in addition to the written text of the Pentateuch, God revealed at Mount Sinai the Oral Torah, which is of equal sanctity and authority. Following this approach, it was suggested that it was easy to get the Israelites' unconditional consent to the finite-looking corpus of the written Torah.

Not all the Hebrews, however, were so ready to commit themselves to the Oral Torah, a vast body of lore that encompasses the classical literature of the Talmud, commentaries and codes, infinitely expanding and developing through the generations. It was with respect to this branch of the Torah that the Almighty was required to resort to threats and coercion.

It is interesting to note that the first known appearance of this interpretation seems to be in a sermon preached in the early Middle Ages, aimed at underlining the interdependence of the Written and Oral Torahs. It is clear that the homelist was responding to an actual challenge: This was the era which marked the rise of the Karaite movement, a Jewish sect that claimed to accept only the written Bible, and to reject the authority of the rabbinic-talmudic traditions. Our anonymous commentator was saying, in effect, that the same problem had existed in the time of Moses, and that the response had to be forceful and decisive.

Other midrashic interpretations of the Sinai revelation have also been explained as reactions to sectarian challenges.

For example, in one talmudic passage Rabbi Yohanan stated that when Israel stood before Mount Sinai they became cleansed of the filth that had been injected into Eve by the serpent in the Garden of Eden (*Shabbat* 146a). This strange-sounding comment takes on new meaning when we contrast it to the Christian teachings of the apostle Paul, who argued that the Torah was powerless to cure people of the "original sin" of Adam and Eve; only through the acceptance of Christianity could such purification be realized. In fact, according to this view, all the "Law" [i.e., the Torah] did was magnify people's consciousness of sin. Rabbi Yohanan is countering such arguments by saying that, whatever defilement may have attached itself to humanity, it was removed at Mount Sinai by virtue of the acceptance of God's Torah. Ironically, in Rabbi Yohanan's version only the Jews were cleansed. The heathen nations, who had not been present to accept the Torah, remained in their spiritual impurity.

A final note: The legend of the lifting up of Mount Sinai makes its appearance in an unexpected place: the Qur'an. According to Muslim belief, this work, the sacred scripture of Islam, contains the revelations spoken to the prophet Muhammad (570–632 C.E.). It is a work that is deeply influenced by Jewish teachings.

The Qur'an provides a lengthy description of the story of the Israelite Exodus. It includes this passage, in which God is said to relate:

> *And then We took a covenant with you and raised the mountain over you: Accept forcefully what We have given you, and remember what is in it. (Sura II, 60)*

Most of the Muslim commentators, who could find no basis for this story in the biblical text itself, and who were of course not experts in talmudic writings, insisted that the passage must be understood figuratively.

The commentators might have been tipped off, however, to Muhammad's use of a Jewish source by his choice of words. In the *sura* cited above, for the word "mountain" he uses not the expected Arabic term *jabal*, but an Aramaic equivalent: *tura. Tura* is also the word that is employed to translate "mountain" in the standard Jewish Aramaic translations of the Torah.

Jewish readers, at any rate, can easily discern the influence on the Qur'an of the rabbinic traditions we have been discussing.

SUGGESTIONS FOR FURTHER READING

Katsh, Abraham Isaac. *Judaism and the Koran: Biblical and Talmudic Backgrounds of the Koran and its Commentaries.* Perpetua Books. New York: A.S. Barnes, 1962.

Scholem, G. G. *Jewish Gnosticism, Merkabah Mysticism, and Talmudic Tradition.* New York, Jewish Theological Seminary of America, 1965.

Urbach, E. *The Sages: Their Concepts and Beliefs.* Cambridge, MA. and London: Harvard University Press, 1987.

Renewing the Covenant at Qumran*

Students of talmudic law and of Second Temple Jewish history are acutely aware of the ongoing dispute between rival Jewish movements about how to calculate the date of Shavu'ot. The Torah speaks of counting seven weeks beginning on "the morrow of the sabbath." Jews today interpret this law in accordance with the view of the ancient Pharisees, that "sabbath" here refers to the first day of Passover, causing Shavu'ot to fall fifty days later, on the sixth day of Sivan.

The Talmud relates that other Jewish groups at the time understood "sabbath" in its normal sense of Saturday. Thus, they began their fifty-day count from a Sunday during or after Passover, and invariably celebrated Shavu'ot on a Sunday seven weeks afterwards (*Menahot* 65a).

The Dead Sea Scrolls have enriched our knowledge of this dispute, by showing us that according to the calendar of the ancient Essene sect, the counting invariably commenced on the Sunday following the end of Passover,

* *The Jewish Free Press*, Calgary, May 2, 2002, pp. 8–9.

the twenty-sixth of Nissan, and culminated with the festival of Shavu'ot on Sunday the fifteenth of Sivan.

The respective methods of calculation gave rise to conflicting appreciations of the festival's significance. The Torah itself describes Shavu'ot only as an agricultural holiday that commemorates the grain harvest (Leviticus 23:15–22). According to the Pharisaic-rabbinic system, however, the date of Shavu'ot coincides with that of the revelation of the Torah at Mount Sinai. Only in this way does Shavu'ot acquire a historical meaning as the anniversary of that central moment in the Jewish past when Israel entered into a covenant with God by agreeing to obey the laws of the Torah.

It would appear to follow naturally from all these premises that the advocates of the Dead Sea calendar did not possess an annual festival to commemorate the revelation at Sinai.

This would indeed follow naturally – but it is apparently not true.

The Dead Sea Scrolls contain precise guidelines for the celebration of Shavu'ot as the festival of the Renewal of the Covenant. This holiday seems to have occupied a vital place in their religious life. It was not a mere matter of adding special prayers or biblical readings. To all appearances, the festival ritual involved a solemn re-enacting of the ceremony described in the Book of Deuteronomy Chapter 27, when the people positioned themselves between Mount Ebal and Mount Gerizim, while the priests intoned the blessings in store for those who observe the covenant; and the Levites uttered the blood-curdling curses that will befall those who violate that covenant. To each declaration, the participants responded "Amen."

The Essene holiday incorporated ingredients from yet another momentous ceremony from biblical history, when the returning Babylonian exiles congregated in Jerusalem to accept upon themselves the obligations of the Torah. Like that earlier assembly, described in the Book of Nehemiah (Chapter 9), the Essene covenant renewal included the recitation of a survey of Jewish history that highlighted God's generous providence towards his people, contrasting it with the sad record of backsliding and ingratitude that culminated in the destruction of their sanctuary and exile from their homeland.

The texts give us the impression that the participants in the ceremony were expected to line themselves up in single file and pass between the priests and the Levites.

Other elements in the ritual included the uttering of blessings to the God of goodness and the heaping of vigorous curses upon the evil power of Belial.

It is consistent with the sect's general outlook that good and evil are not portrayed as options between which the individual may choose. On the contrary, Essene theology held that humanity has already been pre-assigned into opposing domains of good and evil. Members of the sect have, virtually by definition, been designated to the realm of goodness and light, whereas the rest of the world are counted among the Children of Darkness.

Accordingly, those who take part in the covenant renewal ceremony are not declaring their personal determination to choose good over evil, but merely expressing their appreciation that the Almighty placed them under the powers of goodness, rather than the forces of Belial to which the rest of the world is subject.

Although the talmudic tradition understood that the ceremony at Mount Ebal and Mount Gerizim had been a one-time event performed when the Israelites first entered the Promised Land, the Essenes seemed to have perceived it as an annual holiday. To be precise, the scrolls stipulate that the ceremony must be repeated every year "throughout the days of the dominion of Belial." That is evidently another way of saying that the renewal ceremony is necessary only as long as humanity continues to inhabit an imperfect and unredeemed world. By implication, the ritual will become obsolete after God has vanquished the forces of darkness and vindicated the small community of his faithful. The Qumran community, like many other Jews of the time, lived in imminent anticipation of this great event.

The designers of the covenant ceremony were aware that membership in the Essene community did not constitute an automatic guarantee of personal holiness or religious virtue. For this reason, apparently, reference is made in the scrolls to two classes of individuals who, in spite of their ostensible belonging to the Dead Sea community, will not benefit from the blessings that accrue to the true Children of Light. One such group consists of people who avoid participating in the ceremony in the hope that they can thereby evade the obligations and penalties that would arise from fully accepting the conditions of the covenant. The second group included people who went through all the outward motions of accepting the covenant, but remained insincere in their commitment. Special curses are reserved for both these groupings. They are declared to be impure and subject to terrible divine chastisement.

The dire and fatalistic mood that radiates from the Dead Sea Scrolls strikes an extreme contrast with the joy and optimism that permeate the rabbinic celebration of Shavu'ot. Although few of us will be induced to convert to the Essene brand of Judaism, I believe that we can still be moved by the sect's devotion to the Torah as they understood it, and by their earnest efforts to keep Jewish tradition alive and meaningful.

Suggestions for Further Reading

Licht, Jacob, ed. *The Rule Scroll: A Scroll from the Wilderness of Judea.* Jerusalem: Bialik Institute, 1965.

Milik, J. T. *Ten Years of Discovery in the Wilderness of Judaea.* 1st English ed. Studies in Biblical Theology. London: SCM Press, 1959.

Vermès, Géza. *Discovery in the Judean Desert.* New York: Desclee, 1956.

———. *The Complete Dead Sea Scrolls in English.* London: Penguin, 1995.

Glossary

Note: Basic information about the various holidays may be found at the beginnings of the respective sections of the book.

Abravanel, Isaac (1437–1508)

Served as statesman and financier to rulers of Portugal, Spain and – after the expulsion of Jews from the Iberian peninsula – Naples and Venice. He was the prolific author of works on Jewish philosophy, theology history, and biblical interpretation.

Adar

Hebrew month in which Purim occurs (around February and March).

Afikoman

Hebrew, from Greek *epikomon*. In the Mishnah: Revelry following a banquet, a practice that the Mishnah forbids after the Passover meal.

In later usage: a piece of matzah that must be eaten as the final item of the Passover meal.

Agrippa

One of two kings of Judea toward the end of the Second Commonwealth era: Agrippa I (c.10 B.C.E.–44 C.E.); Agrippa II (27–100 C.E.).

Akiva, Rabbi

Foremost Jewish sage of the early second century C.E., he developed a distinctive system of biblical interpretation and established the foundations for the Mishnah. A supporter of the Bar Kokhba revolt in 132–35, he was martyred by the Romans for teaching Torah in defiance of the official prohibition.

Al ha-Nissim

Hebrew: "For the miracles ..." An addition to the regular prayers on Purim and Hanukkah that recounts the events that are commemorated on those holidays.

Alkabetz, Rabbi Solomon ben Moses Hallevi

A member of the sixteenth-century Kabbalistic circle in Safed, Israel, Alkabetz was the author of liturgical hymns and an extensive commentary to the Book of Esther.

Apocalypse

Greek: "secret." A popular genre of Jewish religious literature during the Second Commonwealth and Roman eras, in which a biblical figure is given a symbolic vision of the end of history, usually involving the catastrophic destruction of the evil heathen empires.

Apocrypha

Greek: "hidden." Books that were included in the Alexandrian Greek Jewish scriptures, but not accepted as part of the standard Jewish Bible.

Arama, Rabbi Isaac ben Moses (ca. 1420–1494)

Distinguished Spanish Jewish thinker and exegete, known chiefly for his *Akedat Yitshak*, a philosophical commentary to the Torah.

Ashkenaz [English adjective: Ashkenazic]

Taken from the name of an obscure nation mentioned in the Bible (Genesis 10:2), the term was adopted in the Middle Ages to designate Germany. It is used principally to refer to the Jews of Germany and their successors in eastern Europe, America, and other lands. Ashkenazic Jews evolved their own ritual customs and developed their distinctive vernacular, Yiddish.

Auto-da-fé

Portuguese: "Act of the faith." The burning of alleged heretics at the stake by the Spanish Inquisition.

Blessing

The basic unit of the Hebrew liturgy, usually beginning with the formula "Blessed are you, Lord God ..." Hebrew: B'rakhah.

Book of the Pious (Sefer Hasidim)

An important compendium of the teachings of the Hasidei Ashkenaz pietistic movement in medieval Germany, including teachings by Rabbi Samuel ben Kalonymus, Judah ben Samuel the Pious, and Eleazar ben Judah.

Cantillation

The traditional manner of chanting biblical texts in the synagogue. A very precise system of musical signs (which also indicate the syntax) are included in codices and books, but are not written in the handwritten scrolls that are used in the synagogue service.

Chabad-Lubavitch

A branch of Hasidism founded in Lithuania by Rabbi Shneur Zalman of Liady, noted for its combination of mystical fervor and traditional scholarship.

Chajes, Rabbi Zvi Hirsch (1805–55)

A Galician rabbi who was instrumental in promoting moderate traditionalism through his combination of traditional talmudic erudition and a knowledge of European culture.

Converso

Spanish: "convert." Jews of Spain and Portugal who converted to Christianity under the threats of the Inquisition, but continued to observe Judaism in secret. A less offensive term than the more familiar, but offensive "Marrano" [= pig].

Dead Sea Scrolls

A library of several hundred manuscripts, most of them in severely fragmented form, discovered at Khirbet Qumran and some other sites in the Judean desert. The scrolls contain a representative collection of the Jewish literature from the late Second Commonwealth era, especially the writings of the Essene sect.

Edom

A nation that inhabited the southern territories of the Land of Israel. According to the Bible, the Edomites were descended from Jacob's brother Esau, who was also known as Edom.

Eiger, Rabbi Akiva (1761–1837)

Prominent German rabbi who served much of his career in Posen. He composed important collections of responsa, and was the father-in-law of Rabbi Moses Schreiber, the "Hasam Sofer."

Emancipation

The movement to grant Jews full rights as individual citizens in modern European societies.

Emden, Rabbi Jacob (1697–1776)

A prominent German rabbi with a broad interest in science and general studies. Emden became the rabbi of Altona, and was a determined opponent of the Sabbatian movement.

Eretz Israel

Hebrew: "the Land of Israel." The homeland of the Jewish people.

Essenes

A Jewish sect of the Second Commonwealth era who opposed the prevailing religious leadership in Jerusalem and established a community in the Judean desert where they lived according to their own strict interpretation of Judaism. It is widely assumed that the community at Qumran, where the Dead Sea Scroll library was housed, was an Essene settlement.

Esther (Book of)

The biblical book describing how a Jewish woman named Esther saved the Jewish people from extermination by becoming the Queen of Persia. The events related in Esther are commemorated on Purim, when the book is read publicly in the synagogue.

Etrog

A citron, a yellow fruit that is used in celebrating the holiday of Sukkot.

Exilarch

The official head of the Babylonian Jewish community during talmudic and early medieval times.

Feinstein, Rabbi Moses (1895–1986)

The most prominent authority on Orthodox Jewish religious law during the twentieth century. Born in Belorussia, Rabbi Feinstein spent most of his life in New York City.

Ga'on

From Hebrew: "pride." The title given to the head of the rabbinic academies in Babylonia and the Land of Israel during the early Islamic era.

In medieval times, the title was occasionally attached to certain distinguished rabbis, such as Rabbi Nissim Ibn Shahin of Kairowan (eleventh century), and especially Rabbi Elijah of Vilna (1720–97). In contemporary usage, it is common to attach the honorific "Ga'on" to the name of almost any rabbi.

Ge'onic

The English adjective derived from *Ga'on*.

Genizah

According to Jewish law it is forbidden to actively destroy or discard sacred texts. Religious books that have become unusable are placed in special depositories (usually in synagogues), where they are allowed to decompose naturally. Often, after the depositories become filled, they are transferred to a cemetery for interment in the earth. Such a depository (which can be an entire room or a simple box) is referred to in Hebrew as a *genizah*.

The Cairo Genizah was established in the twelfth century in a synagogue in Fustat, the Egyptian capital. Because of the dry climate that retarded decomposition, and their inclusive definition of what constitutes a sacred text (virtually anything written in the Hebrew alphabet, as was the custom among Arabic-speaking Jews even for simple business documents), the Cairo Genizah accumulated hundreds of thousands of texts, most of them in a fragmentary state. The

Genizah is not limited to literary works, but contains personal letters, business contracts, and other invaluable records of daily life. It continued to be actively used until the late nineteenth century, when Solomon Schechter realized its importance and brought its remaining contents to Cambridge University. The study of the Genizah manuscripts has revolutionized virtually every area of ancient and medieval Jewish studies.

Gimatria

Hebrew, from the Greek: "geometria"; i.e., mathematics. Numerology, a traditional Jewish expository method based on finding patterns in the numerical values assigned to the letters of Hebrew words.

Graetz, Heinrich (1817–91)

German Jewish scholar, pioneer of modern Jewish historical research. Graetz composed the first comprehensive survey of Jewish history.

Gur

An influential Hasidic sect founded by R. Isaac Meir Alter (1789–1866) and led by his descendants. The sect is named for the Polish town where it originated. After the Holocaust, its centre of activities moved to Israel.

Gut Yontef

Yiddish greeting: "Good holiday!"

Haftarah (plural: Haftarot)

Hebrew: "conclusion." A passage from the Prophets section of the Bible that is recited in the synagogue after the reading from the Torah on Sabbaths and holidays. The haftarah selection usually shares a common theme with the day's Torah section.

Haggadah

Hebrew: "telling." Usually: the liturgy for the Passover night meal (seder) in which the story of the Exodus from Egypt is expounded, in observance of the precept (Exodus 13:8) "And you shall tell your child on that day ..."

Halakhah (English adjective: "halakhic")

Apparently derived from the Hebrew word for "walking," this term is used to designate the component of rabbinic activity and literature that deals with the derivation and application of religious law. Thus, an authority on Jewish religious law can be referred to in English as a "halakhist."

Hallel

Hebrew: "praise." Psalms 113–118, recited or sung on joyous festivals.

Hasidism

From the Hebrew: "piety." A religious revival movement that arose in eastern Europe in the latter eighteenth century under the charismatic leadership of Rabbi Israel ben Eliezer of Medzibozh, know as the "Ba'al Shem Tov" or "Besht." Hasidism incorporated many elements of previous Jewish religiosity but was distinguished by its preference for spontaneous religious fervour over scholarly erudition and talmudic study. Hasidism formulated a popular mystical doctrine based on the Kabbalah, and stressed forms of religious expression that could be observed by the common and uneducated classes, a fact that provoked opposition from the scholarly religious leadership.

Later generations of Hasidism adopted a charismatic model of leadership in which local leaders served as spiritual intermediaries and were revered as supernatural wonder-workers.

Hasidut Ashkenaz

Hebrew: "German pietism." An ascetic Jewish movement whose adherents sought to attain an ideal saintly character. They formulated mystical approaches to meditation on prayer, and a theology that stressed the divine "glory," the intermediary between humans and the unknowable God. Members of this movement are called *Hasidei Ashkenaz.*

Hasmoneans

The priestly family who led a successful uprising against the Seleucid Greeks in the early second century B.C.E. They took on the offices of monarchs and High Priest, and their dynasty held power until deposed by the Romans in 63 B.C.E.

Heavenly Court

In the imagery of the rabbis, God presides over a celestial court (often modelled after a Roman tribunal) to judge humanity, especially at Rosh Hashanah and Yom Kippur.

Herod (73–74 B.C.E.)

Of Idumean (Edomite) origin, Herod "the Great" was a Roman puppet monarch who held tyrannical sway over Judea. His reign was characterised by ruthless and paranoiac suppression of potential opposition, but also by an ambitious program of public works and buildings, including a magnificent new Jerusalem Temple.

Heschel, Abraham Joshua (1907–72)

An important Jewish philosopher and teacher. Heir to a European Hasidic tradition, Heschel escaped to America during the Holocaust and was a member of the faculty of the Jewish Theological Seminary in New York. His writings combined Hasidic themes, such as the personal relationships between humans and God, with modern existentialist ideas. He was also a political and social activist, involved in the American Civil Rights movement and the opposition to the Vietnam war.

High Holy Days

Rosh Hashanah and Yom Kippur.

Hirsch, Rabbi Samson Raphael (1808–88)

A German rabbi and thinker, Hirsch formulated an ideology of "Neo-Orthodoxy" which combined a conservative theology and inflexible standard of religious observance with a positive attitude towards those aspects of modern European culture that did not pose religious threats to Judaism. A determined opponent of the Reform Movement, he initiated the secession of Frankfurt's Orthodox minority from the larger Jewish community, which was under Reform leadership.

Hol ha-Mo'ed

Hebrew: "non-sacred parts of festivals." The intermediate days of Passover and Sukkot, which are observed as holy days, but are not subject to all the ritual restrictions that apply on full holy days.

Hoshana

Hebrew: "Save us." A procession observed during Sukkot in which worshippers march around the synagogue (originally, in the Jerusalem Temple) reciting poetic litanies based on the Hebrew expression *Hoshana*. The term also designates the genre of liturgical poems. See Psalms 118:25.

Ibn Ezra, Rabbi Abraham ben Meir (c. 1089 – c. 1164.)

Originally from Tudela, Spain, Ibn Ezra spent much of his life wandering in poverty through Europe and the Middle East. He excelled as a poet, astrologer, Neoplatonic philosopher, grammarian and biblical exegete. His biblical commentators are distinguished for his careful attention to issues of grammar and lexicography.

Ibn Habib, Rabbi Jacob (c. 1445–1516)
Sixteenth-century rabbi, a Spanish refugee who settled in Salonica, and is best known for his *'Ein Ya'akov*, a collection of all the Aggadah (non-legal material) in the Talmud

Idumean
= Edomite

Inquisition
An agency established by the Roman Catholic church to convict and punish heretics, including converted Jews who were continuing to practice Judaism. The Inquisition was infamous for its cruel tortures and rapacious seizure of property.

Isaac of Dampierre
A nephew of Rabbi Jacob Tam, he lived in France during the twelfth century, and was one of the most prolific authors of the Tosafot.

Isserles, Rabbi Moses (1530–1572)
Polish authority on Jewish Law, known chiefly for the glosses he composed to Rabbi Joseph Karo's *Shulhan 'Arukh* to include the traditions of Ashkenazic Jews.

Jewish National Fund (JNF)
An agency of the Zionist movement established in 1901 to purchase land on behalf of the Jewish people and to make the land of Israel suitable for settlement and cultivation.

Josephus Flavius (c. 38–after 100)
A first-century Jew of priestly descent who served as a military commander in the Jewish uprising against Rome and defected to the Romans towards the end of the war. Under Roman protection, he composed several historical and polemical works in Greek that are

among the most important records we have of Jewish history and religion during the Second Temple era.

Judah Hallevi (c. 1075–1141)

Spanish poet and theologian, famous for his *Kuzari*, a philosophical dialogue in defence of Judaism, and for his exquisite Hebrew poems, especially those expressing his longing for the Land of Israel. At the peak of his success, he gave up his comfortable life in Spain to migrate to the Holy Land via Egypt.

Judah ben Samuel the Pious (1150–1217)

Leading figure and teacher of the Hasidei Ashkenaz pietist circle. Much of his teaching is embedded in the *Book of the Pious.*

Judah [ben Ilai], Rabbi

References to "Rabbi Judah" in the Mishnah or Talmud are to Rabbi Judah ben Ilai, a disciple of Rabbi Akiva who was himself a prominent teacher in the Land of Israel during the mid-second century.

Kabbalah [Kabbalist, Kabbalistic, etc.]

Hebrew: "received tradition." An esoteric interpretation of Judaism based on a symbolic structure of ten emanated powers (*sefirot*) through which the unknowable God created and guides the universe, and through which humans can interact with the divine realms. Kabbalistic doctrine is first attested in southern France and Spain in the twelfth century. Kabbalists utilize the symbolism of the ten sefirot to provide profound allegorical interpretation of the Bible and other classic Jewish texts and to attach metaphysical significance to the observance of Jewish commandments and laws.

The term "Kabbalah" is often employed in a more general way to designate all manifestations of Jewish mysticism.

Karaites

"Scripturalists." a Jewish movement that arose in the eighth century, claiming to acknowledge only the authority of the Bible, while rejecting the oral tradition that was advocated by the rabbis and embodied in the Mishnah and Talmud.

Kosher

Hebrew: "fit; proper." Usually employed to designate food that is permissible for consumption in accordance with the Jewish dietary rules.

Kuzari

Theological classic by Rabbi Judah Hallevi, demonstrating the superiority of the Jewish religion. The Kuzari is constructed as a dialogue between the king of the Khazars (a west Asian nation whose ruler adopted Judaism in the ninth century) and a Jewish scholar.

Landsmanschaft (plural: Landsmanschaften)

German and Yiddish: An organization of immigrants from the same country or town.

Leviathan

A great sea creature mentioned in the Bible. In later Jewish legend it was said that the leviathan would be served to the righteous at a banquet in the Next World.

Lulav

An unopened palm branch that is carried and waved as one of the "four species" of plants in the rituals of the Sukkot holiday. See Leviticus 23:40.

Luria, Rabbi Isaac (1534–72) (also known by the acronym "ARI")

Visionary whose interpretation of the Kabbalah was accepted as the definitive one for subsequent generations. Luria was a native of Israel who did not write any books of his own. His entire career as a Kabbalistic teacher occurred during the last three years of his life in Safed.

Maccabee, Judah

The eldest son of Mattathias the Hasomonean priest, Judah was the brilliant general who waged a victorious guerrilla campaign against Antiochus IV's armies, driving them out of Jerusalem. He died in battle in 160 B.C.E. and was succeeded by his brother Jonathan. The epithet "Maccabee" means "hammer," referring perhaps to his military power or his physical shape.

Maccabees, books of

Ancient books, included in the Apocrypha, that describe the revolt led by the Hasmoneans against the Greeks and the events that are commemorated on the festival of Hanukkah.

Maharil, acronym for: Rabbi Jacob Moelin (c. 1365–1427)

A rabbi in Mayence, Germany, whose writings are among the most important sources of information on the liturgical customs of Ashkenazic Jewry. His personal practices were recorded meticulously by a disciple in the work entitled "Sefer [the book of] Maharil."

Maharsha, acronym for: Rabbi Samuel Eidels (1555–1631)

An important Polish commentator on the Talmud.

Maimonides, Rabbi Moses (1135–204)

Rabbi Moses ben Maimon, known also by his Hebrew acronym Rambam, was one of the most prominent and influential Jewish scholars of the all time. Born in Spain, his family fled persecution settling in Fustat (Cairo), Egypt, where he was active as physician, scholar, and community leader. Maimonides formulated a controversial integration of traditional Judaism and Aristotelian philosophy. His major works include: his Arabic commentary to the Mishnah; his enumeration of the 613 Commandments of the Torah; the *Mishneh Torah,* a comprehensive and systematic codification of all of Jewish law; and the *Guide of the Perplexed,* his philosophical masterpiece.

Matriarchs

The female ancestors of the Jewish people according to the Bible: Sarah, Rebecca, Rachel, and Leah.

Matzah [plural: matzot]

Hebrew: Unleavened bread, consumed on the biblical festival of Passover (Exodus 12:39; 13:6, etc.).

Megillah

Hebrew: "scroll." Most commonly used to designate the scroll of the biblical Book of Esther, which is read publicly on Purim.

Menorah

Hebrew: "candelabrum." A seven-branch candelabrum stood in the Jerusalem Temple. A nine-branched candelabrum (with candles for the eight nights of the holiday and the extra "shammash" light) is used on Hanukkah.

Meron

A village in the Galilee that is the traditional burial place of Rabbi Simeon ben Yohai. It is the centre of a popular celebration (*hillula*) on the anniversary of Rabbi Simeon's death (Lag ba-'Omer).

Messiah (English adjective: messianic)

From the Hebrew: "anointed." In biblical times, the ceremonies for installing priests and kings involved the ritual anointing of their heads with olive oil. Hence, the vision of restored Jewish sovereignty in a redeemed future came to be associated with the figure of an anointed monarch from the line of King David, who will rule over an ideal and united Israel in the end of days.

Mezuzah [plural: mezuzot]

Hebrew: "doorpost." A parchment containing texts from the Torah that is attached to the doorposts of Jewish homes.

Midrash

The component of ancient rabbinic teachings and literature that is related to the Bible. The term "Midrash" (from a root meaning "search, seek") can refer to the method of interpretation, to the teachings themselves, or to the collections and books in which they appear. Midrash can be exegetical, focusing on the systematic interpretation of biblical texts, or homiletic, artistically using biblical quotations to fashion an structured literary sermon.

Minhah

Hebrew: "gift." Although the term originally designated meal-offerings, it is most commonly used as the name of the daily afternoon prayer service.

Miracle of oil

According to a legend found only in the Babylonian Talmud, when the Hasmoneans liberated the Jerusalem Temple from the Greeks, they found only a tiny cruse of pure oil with which to light the menorah, with enough oil for only one day. However, it miraculously lasted for eight days until a fresh supply could be obtained. For this reason, Hanukkah is celebrated for eight days.

Mishnah

A collection of traditions, assembling the decisions and opinions of Jewish sages, mostly from the first two centuries C.E. Composed in Hebrew, the Mishnah classifies the major areas of Jewish religious law into six main topics ("orders"), which are in turn subdivided into some sixty treatises ("tractates"). The Mishnah is differentiated from other collections produced at the time by the fact that it follows a logical, topical order, rather than expounding the Bible. The definitive version of the Mishnah was compiled orally by Rabbi Judah Ha-Nasi early in the third century, at which point it became a source of religious authority and a topic of study for subsequent generations of Jewish scholars.

Musaf

Hebrew: "additional." Originally, this referred to the additional sacrifices that were offered on festivals. Now it is most commonly used to designate the additional prayer services that are added to the festivals.

Nahman [ben Jacob], Rav (died 320)

A Babylonian rabbi and judge.

Nahmanides, Rabbi Moses (1194–1270)

Rabbi Moses ben Nahman, known also by his Hebrew acronym Ramban, lived in Gerona in Christian Catalonia. Although he was a fiercely independent thinker, he was also a religious conservative who defended established beliefs and institutions against new ideas. Following his participation in the disputation of Barcelona of 1263, he emigrated to the Holy Land in 1267.

Nahmanides contributed to many areas of Jewish thought and scholarship. His major works include: an incisive commentary on the Torah (including some Kabbalistic interpretations); analytical commentaries on the Talmud; and many volumes of responsa, sermons, and ethical works.

Nasi

Hebrew: "Prince; patriarch." The title given to the leader of the Jewish supreme court (Sanhedrin) and Israeli community during the talmudic era. During the earlier part of the era the Nasi was expected to combine political and religious scholarly authority, though it later became more of a political office.

Nissan

The first month of the Hebrew calendar, when Passover occurs. Nissan always occurs in Spring.

Numerology

See: Gimatria.

Orthodox Judaism

The streams of modern Judaism that are opposed to major changes in practice or belief and are committed to traditional Jewish law as embodied in codes like the *Shulkah Arukh*.

Parashah [plural: parshiyot]

Hebrew: "section." A section of the Bible, especially the portion of the Torah designated to be read on a specific Sabbath according to the annual sequence of readings.

Patriarchs

The male ancestors of the Jewish people according to the Bible: Abraham, Isaac and Jacob.

Pharisee/Pharisaic

A movement in Second Commonwealth Judaism that advocated scholarly excellence (as distinct from priestly pedigree) as a key virtue of Jewish authority, and accepted the authority of an oral tradition in addition to that of the Torah.

Pinto, Rabbi Josiah (1565–1648)
Syrian rabbi and preacher, author or an important commentary on Rabbi Jacob Ibn Habib's *'Ein Ya'akov.*

Piyut
Hebrew, from the Greek "poetes": poet. Hebrew liturgical poetry, elaborate literary versions of the prayers.

Purim-shpiel
Yiddish: "Purim play." A theatrical production, often of a satirical nature or on a biblical theme, performed on the Purim holiday. Purim-shpiels were popular in many Ashkenazic communities, especially in Poland.

Pushkah
Yiddish: a coin-box for charity.

Qumran
The archaeological site in the Judean desert near where many of the Dead Sea Scrolls were discovered in caves; believed to have been a settlement of the Essene sect.

Rabbah [Rav Abba bar Nahmani] (died 330)
An important Babylonian rabbi, head of the academy at Pumbedita.

Rabbi [English adjectives: rabbinic, rabbinical]
Hebrew: "my master." A title that came into use towards the end of the first century C.E. to designate an ordained authority on Jewish tradition, authorized to serve as a judge on a religious court and to issue rulings on matters of religious law and practice. In modern times, the rabbi has taken on pastoral functions similar to those of Christian clergy.

Rashi (1041–1105)

Acronym for Rabbi Solomon ben Isaac; the foremost Jewish commentator on the Bible and Babylonian Talmud.

During his student years, Rashi studied with the leading Jewish scholars of Germany and France, but lived most of his life in Troyes, northern France, where he earned his living in the wine trade. Rashi's commentaries on the Bible, especially on the Torah, present a variety of traditional and scholarly approaches, incorporating many interpretations from the Talmud and midrashic works.

Rashi's commentaries occupy a central place in traditional Jewish learning and are considered the standard explanations through which Jews approach their authoritative religious texts.

Rav

An alternative form for the title "Rabbi," especially for Babylonian teachers of the talmudic era.

Rav [Abba Arikha] (died 247)

A Babylonian scholar who studied in the Land of Israel and returned to Babylonia to become one of the foundational figures of the Babylonian rabbinate.

Reform Judaism

A movement that began in modern European communities and aims to introduce changes into Judaism in order to make it more consistent with the values, beliefs, and circumstances of the modern world.

Rokeah, Rabbi Eleazar (c. 1176–1238)

A rabbi in Worms, Germany, he was an important representative of the Hasidut Ashkenaz movement. Author of many works, including commentaries on the mystical meanings of the Hebrew prayers.

Rosh Hodesh
Hebrew: "the head of the month." The beginning of a lunar month according to the Hebrew calendar.

Sa'adia Ga'on [Sa'adiah ben Joseph al-Fayumi (882–942)]
Originally from Egypt, Sa'adia was appointed Ga'on, head of the Sura academy in Baghdad. He was a pioneer in several areas of Jewish religious life, including systematic theology, liturgical poetry, biblical studies (he composed an important Arabic translation of the Bible), and jurisprudence. Sa'adia took part in several polemical struggles, notably as a champion of the Babylonian religious leadership over that of the Land of Israel; and of talmudic Judaism against the challenges of the Karaites.

Sabbatian
English adjective: related to Shabbetai Zvi or his messianic movement.

Sabbatical year
According to the Torah, the land of Israel observes a "Sabbath" every seven years: fields must be left fallow, produce is treated as ownerless, debts are cancelled, etc.

Sadducees
A Jewish sect of the Second Temple era representing the interests of the priestly leadership of the Zadokite dynasty. They tended towards a literal reading of the Torah and stressed the importance of the Temple and its cult.

Safed
A town in northern Israel on a hill overlooking the Sea of Galilee, Safed achieved prominence in the sixteenth century as the centre of a Kabbalistic community.

Samaritans

The inhabitants of the area of Samaria, on the west bank of the Jordan river, who observe a religion similar to Judaism, based on the Torah and the Book of Joshua. the Samaritans have their cultic centre in Nablus, near Mount Gerizim. The Bible (see 2 Kings 17) relates that they originated as foreign exiles who were transferred there by the Assyrians after the expulsion of the Israelite populace. The Samaritans themselves claim to be the remnants of the original Israelites who were never sent into exile.

Schreiber (Sofer), Rabbi Moses (1763–1838)

Originally from Frankfort a/M, he served as rabbi in Pressburg, Hungary. He is usually referred to by the title of his influential responsa collection: *Hasam Sofer*. Rabbi Schreiber was a staunch opponent of all expressions of modernism and reform.

Second Jewish Commonwealth

The era in Jewish history extending from the return of the Babylonian exiles to Judea (c. 536 B.C.E.) until the destruction of Jerusalem by the Romans in 70 C.E.

Second Temple

The exclusive centre of sacrificial worship in Jerusalem, built by the returning exiles from Babylonia and subsequently expanded significantly by Herod in 19–63 C.E. The term is also used to express the historical era when the Temple stood, and is equivalent to "Second Commonwealth."

Seder

Hebrew: "order." The ritual meal held on the first nights of Passover, in which the story of the Exodus from Egypt is expounded and the experiences of slavery and liberation are relived through diverse symbolic actions and foods.

Sepharad (English adjective: Sepharadic)

A biblical term referring to Spain and used to designate the Jews of Spain and other Arabic-speaking or Muslim countries during the Middle Ages, or Jewish communities whose ancestors fled from Spain or Portugal after the expulsion in 1492.

Shabbat

Hebrew: the Sabbath.

Shabbetai Zvi (1626–1676)

A native of Smyrna, Turkey, he was the leader of a messianic movement that attracted an immense following in the Jewish world. Fuelled by Kabbalistic doctrines, the movement continued to thrive even after Shabbetai Zvi himself had converted to Islam under threat of death by the Turkish sultan.

Shammai and Hillel, Houses of

Two schools or Jewish law during the first century C.E. Hundreds of disputes between the two schools are cited in rabbinic literature. In most (but not all) cases, the House of Shammai takes a more stringent position and the House of Hillel a more lenient one.

Shammash

An extra candle used to kindle the obligatory eight flames on Hanukkah. Because it is forbidden to derive benefit from the sacred lights, the shammash is kept lit so that any benefit is perceived as being derived from it.

Sherira ben Hanina Ga'on (906–1006 C.E.)

Head of the talmudic academy of Pumbedita, Babylonia, he was a prolific rabbinic scholar, known especially for his *Epistle* on the history of talmudic literature.

Shneur Zalman of Liady, Rabbi (1748–1813)
Lithuanian Jewish scholar and Hasidic leader, founder of the Habad stream of Hasidism.

Shofar
A ram's horn, whose trumpet-like sound is intoned as the main religious ritual on Rosh Hashanah.

Simeon ben Yohai, Rabbi
Second-century rabbi who is quoted frequently in the Mishnah and Talmud. The medieval Kabbalistic tradition portrayed him as a teacher of esoteric lore, the pseudepigraphic author of the Zohar.

Sinai
The mountain in the Sinai desert where, according to the Bible, God revealed the Torah to Israel. The name is also applied to the event of the revelation.

Sukkah
Hebrew: "booth; tabernacle." A temporary structure in which Jews are required to dwell in observance of the biblical autumn holiday of Sukkot (Tabernacles; see Leviticus 23:42–43).

Synagogue
Greek: "place of assembly." An institution where Jews gather for the recitation of scripture, prayer, study, and other religious or communal purposes.

Talmud
One of two monumental commentaries on the Mishnah collecting the opinions and debates of Jewish religious scholars from the third century C.E. and for several centuries afterward. Two Talmuds have come down to us: the "Jerusalem" or Palestinian Talmud and the

Babylonian. Though the two works are similar in their purpose and structure and contain much common material, it was the Babylonian Talmud that achieved prominence during the Middle Ages and is usually referred to as "the Talmud."

The Talmuds are composed in a combination of Hebrew and Aramaic. They are distinguished by the intricate modes of logical argumentation that the rabbis apply to the interpretation of the Mishnah and to other topics. The opinions of the participating rabbis are subjected to critical scrutiny and logical analysis and are compared to proof-texts from the Bible and other statements by the rabbis.

Although they are organized principally as critical expositions of the religious law of the Mishnah, the Talmuds contain diverse types of material, including biblical exegesis, homiletics, moralistic teachings, case law, legends about biblical figures and rabbis, and much more.

Tam, Rabbi Jacob ben Meir (c. 1100–1171)

French talmudic scholar from the "Tosafot" school, grandson of Rashi. He was one of the most original and unconventional interpreters of the Talmud, known for his bold and ingenious new explanations of Talmud passages.

Tamid

Hebrew: "continual." A sacrifice of a lamb that was to be offered in the Temple on behalf of the community every morning and evening, in accordance with Numbers 28:3–4.

Temple

The sanctuary in Jerusalem that was, according to biblical law, the only place where sacrificial worship might be conducted. The first Temple was built by King Solomon and was destroyed by the Babylonians under Nebuchadnezzar. The second Temple was constructed by the exiles returning from the Babylonian captivity and was destroyed by the Romans in 70 C.E.

T'fillin

Leather boxes containing handwritten passages from the Torah on parchment, which are strapped on the arm and head in fulfillment of the precept to bind God's words "for a sign upon thine hand, and they shall be as frontlets between thine eyes" (Deuteronomy 6:8, etc.). In standard practice, they are worn by men during weekday morning prayers.

T'fillin is often translated incorrectly as "phylacteries," a term that means "amulet" or "good luck charm."

Torah

Hebrew: "teaching" or "instruction." Torah is applied most specifically to the first five books of the Hebrew Bible (also known as the Pentateuch or "Five Books of Moses"), which Jewish tradition regards as the most important and authoritative section of the Bible.

In a more general sense, the term is used to refer to the full range of Jewish religious teaching.

Tosafot

Hebrew: "additions." A school of Talmud commentators in medieval France and Germany (twelfth to fourteenth centuries) known for their critical analyses of selected passages in the Talmud. The name "Tosafot" probably refers to their original function as supplements to Rashi's commentary, since they often propose alternative interpretations to Rashi's. Some of the founders of the school were Rashi's own students and grandchildren.

The typical structure of a Tosafot passage begins with a presentation of Rashi's explanation, then points out a contradiction or logical difficulty and attempts to resolve the problem through a new understanding of the passage and its issues. Tosafot are included in all the standard printed editions of the Talmud.

Tzitzit
Hebrew: "tassels, fringes." Braided tassels attached to the corners of certain garments (e.g., prayer shawls) in accordance with Numbers 15:38–39.

Vital, Rabbi Hayyim (1542–1620)
A member of the mystical circle of Safed whose works on the Kabbalah served as the standard formulation of the doctrines of Rabbi Isaac Luria.

Volozhin
A Lithuanian town that was renowned for its yeshivah founded in 1803 by Rabbi Hayyim Volozhin (1749–1821), which was to become the classic model of Lithuanian yeshivah, a central institution that served as a focus for the finest students throughout the Jewish world. The content of the curriculum emphasized a rigorously logical analysis of the Talmud.

Yadin, Yigael (1917–84)
Israeli archaeologist, general and political figure, known for his dramatic excavations of Massada, the Bar Kokhba remains, and many other major discoveries.

Yahrzeit
German or Yiddish: "anniversary." The annual commemoration of the death of a close relative.

Yavneh [Jamnia]
A coastal town in Judea that became the centre of Jewish religious scholarship and reconstruction in the generations immediately following the destruction of the Second Temple in 70 C.E.

Yeshivah [plural: yeshivot]

Hebrew: A school for advanced religious study, primarily of the Talmud and religious law. In ancient times the primary designation of yeshivah was a court (where religious traditions were debated in order to determine the law).

Yiddish

The vernacular language of Ashkenazic Jews. Primarily a dialect of medieval German, it contains many elements of Hebrew, Aramaic, and various lands through which the Jews migrated.

Yishuv (old or new)

Hebrew: "settlement." One of the Jewish communities in Israel at the beginning of the Zionist migrations. The pre-Zionist "old yishuv" consisted largely of religious Jews who were supported by donations from abroad; the "new yishuv" was more modern and (usually) secular in orientation.

Yohanan [bar Nappaha], Rabbi (died 279)

The most prominent rabbi in the land of Israel during the mid-third century, his teachings are quoted on virtually every page of the Talmud.

Yom Tov

Hebrew: "good day"; i.e., a festival.

Zadokites

Descendants of King Solomon's High Priest Zadok, this dynasty occupied the Jewish High Priesthood through most of the Second Commonwealth, until they were supplanted by the Hasmonean family.

Zionism

The Jewish nationalist movement that arose in the late nineteenth century and proposed to solve the problems of Jewish persecution by creating a national home for the Jewish people in their ancestral homeland.

Zohar

The most widely accepted text of the Kabbalah, this work was composed in Spain in the thirteenth century in the form of midrashic expositions of the Bible, ascribed to Rabbi Simeon ben Yohai and his disciples.

Index

B

C

D

E

F

G

H

I

J

K

L

M

N